International Summit on the Teaching Profession

Schools for 21st-Century Learners

STRONG LEADERS, CONFIDENT TEACHERS, INNOVATIVE APPROACHES

Andreas Schleicher

OECD
BETTER POLICIES FOR BETTER LIVES

This work is published under the responsibility of the Secretary-General of the OECD. The opinions expressed and the arguments employed herein do not necessarily reflect the official views of the OECD member countries.

This document and any map included herein are without prejudice to the status of or sovereignty over any territory, to the delimitation of international frontiers and boundaries and to the name of any territory, city or area.

Please cite this publication as:
Schleicher, A. (2015), *Schools for 21st-Century Learners: Strong Leaders, Confident Teachers, Innovative Approaches*, International Summit on the Teaching Profession, OECD Publishing.
http://dx.doi.org/10.1787/9789264231191-en

ISBN 978-92-64-23118-4 (print)
ISBN 978-92-64-23119-1 (PDF)

Series: International Summit on the Teaching Profession
ISSN 2312-7082 (print)
ISSN 2312-7090 (online)

The statistical data for Israel are supplied by and under the responsibility of the relevant Israeli authorities. The use of such data by the OECD is without prejudice to the status of the Golan Heights, East Jerusalem and Israeli settlements in the West Bank under the terms of international law.

Photo credits:
© AsiaPix/Inmagine
© Jose Luis Pelaez, Inc./Blend Images/Corbis

Corrigenda to OECD publications may be found on line at: *www.oecd.org/publishing/corrigenda*.
© OECD 2015

You can copy, download or print OECD content for your own use, and you can include excerpts from OECD publications, databases and multimedia products in your own documents, presentations, blogs, websites and teaching materials, provided that suitable acknowledgement of OECD as source and copyright owner is given. All requests for public or commercial use and translation rights should be submitted to *rights@oecd.org*. Requests for permission to photocopy portions of this material for public or commercial use shall be addressed directly to the Copyright Clearance Center (CCC) at *info@copyright.com* or the Centre français d'exploitation du droit de copie (CFC) at *contact@cfcopies.com*.

Foreword

The skills that students need to contribute effectively to society are changing constantly, but our education systems are not keeping up. Most schools look much the same today as they did a generation ago, and teachers themselves are often not developing the practices and skills required to meet the diverse needs of today's learners.

What are the skills that young people need to participate fully in this rapidly changing world, and how can education systems best support the kind of teaching that develops those skills? What is the role of teachers in leading innovation, both inside and outside the classroom? What are the different roles and responsibilities of 21st-century school leaders, and how can countries best develop leadership throughout their education systems?

To help governments address these issues, while placing teachers and school leaders at the centre of improvement efforts, the Canadian ministers of education, the OECD and Education International brought education ministers, union leaders and other teacher leaders together for the fifth International Summit on the Teaching Profession in Banff, Canada, in March 2015.

One of the secrets of the success of the International Summit on the Teaching Profession is that it explores difficult and controversial issues on the basis of sound evidence, provided by the OECD as the global leader for internationally comparative data and analysis. This publication summarises the evidence that underpinned the 2015 Summit, bringing together data analysis and experience to develop better education policies for better lives.

The report was prepared by Andreas Schleicher. It is mainly based on data and comparative analysis from several OECD publications: *TALIS 2013 Results: An International Perspective on Teaching and Learning*; *PISA 2012 Results*; and *Innovative Learning Environments*. Julie Bélanger and David Istance provided expert advice, Marilyn Achiron edited the text, and Célia Braga-Schich and Sophie Limoges co-ordinated production of the report.

Table of Contents

EXECUTIVE SUMMARY 9

CHAPTER 1 **BUILDING RESPONSIVE SCHOOLS FOR 21ST-CENTURY LEARNERS** 11

CHAPTER 2 **PROMOTING EFFECTIVE SCHOOL LEADERSHIP** 15
- What school principals do 17
- Sharing responsibilities 19
  Distributed leadership 20
- Defining school goals, programmes and professional development plans 22
- Providing direction to the school and supporting teachers: Instructional leadership 22
  Instructional leadership and school climate 23
- Principals' work experience 24
- Professional development for principals 25
- Principals' job satisfaction 27
- Who are today's school leaders? 29
  Age and gender of principals 29
  Formal education of school principals 30
- Policy implications 34
  Empower teachers to play a role in decision making at the school level 34
  Encourage the practice of distributed leadership 34
  Develop formal programmes to prepare school leaders to enter the profession 35
  Provide opportunities for, and remove barriers to, continuing professional development for principals 35
  Ensure that principals receive training in, and have opportunities to assume, instructional leadership 35

CHAPTER 3 **STRENGTHENING TEACHERS' CONFIDENCE IN THEIR OWN ABILITIES** 39
- Why self-efficacy matters 41
- Teachers' self-efficacy and job satisfaction as related to classroom environment 46
- Teachers' self-efficacy and their relations with colleagues and students 47
  How teachers' relationships with colleagues and students can moderate the influence
  of classroom composition 48
- Teachers' self-efficacy and their professional development 49
- Teachers' self-efficacy and the appraisal and feedback they receive 50
- Teachers' self-efficacy and their beliefs and practices 51
  How teachers' beliefs and practices mediate the impact of classroom composition on their sense
  of self-efficacy and job satisfaction 52
- Teachers' self-efficacy and their professional collaborative practices 53
- Policy implications 55
  Build teachers' capacity to handle misbehaving students 55
  Support the development of interpersonal relationships within the school 56
  Institute meaningful systems of appraisal and feedback that have connections with teachers' practice 56
  Encourage collaboration among teachers, either through professional development activities
  or classroom practices 56

Table of Contents

CHAPTER 4 **INNOVATING TO CREATE 21ST-CENTURY LEARNING ENVIRONMENTS** 61
- Regrouping educators and teachers 62
    - Collaborative planning, orchestration and professional development 63
    - Regrouping teachers to introduce different mixes of learning and pedagogy 63
    - Team teaching to target specific groups of learners 64
    - Enhanced visibility 64
- Regrouping learners 64
    - Grouping together learners of different ages 64
    - Smaller groups within the larger groups 65
- Rescheduling learning: Innovating with how time is used 66
    - Timetables, flexibility and time use 66
    - Organised learning outside regular school hours 67
- Widening pedagogical repertoires 68
    - Inquiry learning 68
    - Authentic learning 69
    - The pedagogical possibilities in "technology-rich" environments 70
    - Mixes of pedagogies 71
- Policy implications 72
    - Create communities and build capacities 73
    - Collaborate and communicate 73
    - Create conditions conducive to innovation 73
    - Ensure coherence 74

This book has...

StatLinks

A service that delivers Excel® files from the printed page!

Look for the *StatLinks* at the bottom left-hand corner of the tables or graphs in this book. To download the matching Excel® spreadsheet, just type the link into your Internet browser, starting with the *http://dx.doi.org* prefix.
If you're reading the PDF e-book edition, and your PC is connected to the Internet, simply click on the link. You'll find *StatLinks* appearing in more OECD books.

BOXES

Box 1.1	The TALIS Design	13
Box 2.1	Promoting teacher leadership in the United States	16
Box 2.2	Description of the principal distributed leadership index	21
Box 2.3	Description of the instructional leadership index	23
Box 2.4	Australia's approach to school leadership and its National Professional Standard for Principals	26
Box 2.5	Description of the principal job satisfaction indices	28
Box 2.6	Sampling school leadership in Denmark	31
Box 2.7	Construction of the leadership training index	32
Box 2.8	Selecting and training school leaders in Singapore	32
Box 2.9	Leadership-preparation programmes in Finland and Norway	33
Box 2.10	Characteristics of exemplary leadership programmes	34
Box 3.1	Teacher self-efficacy and job satisfaction indices	42
Box 3.2	Description of in-school relationships	48
Box 3.3	Teacher development in Finland	50
Box 3.4	Appraisal and feedback measures	50
Box 3.5	The use of teacher and student feedback in Norway	51
Box 3.6	Collaborative evaluation in Denmark	53
Box 3.7	Preparing teachers to lead improvement in Japan	54
Box 4.1	Desirable features of contemporary learning environments	63
Box 4.2	Technology-dependent approaches to teaching and learning	71

FIGURES

Figure 2.1	Principals' working time	17
Figure 2.2	Principals' leadership	18
Figure 2.3	School decisions and collaborative school culture	21
Figure 2.4	Principals' participation in a school development plan	22
Figure 2.5	Work experience of principals	24
Figure 2.6	Principals' recent professional development	25
Figure 2.7	Barriers to principals' participation in professional development	27
Figure 2.8	Principal job satisfaction	29
Figure 2.9	Gender and age distribution of principals	30
Figure 2.10	Elements not included in principals' formal education	31
Figure 2.11	Principals' formal education, including leadership training	33
Figure 3.1	Relationship between the value of the teaching profession and the share of top mathematics performers	40
Figure 3.2	Teachers' view of the way society values the teaching profession	41
Figure 3.3	Teachers' self-efficacy	43
Figure 3.4	Teachers' job satisfaction	45
Figure 3.5	Teachers' job satisfaction and class composition	46
Figure 3.6	The influence of class composition on teachers' attitudes and relationships	48
Figure 3.7	The influence of class composition on teachers' attitudes, beliefs and practices	52
Figure 3.8	Teachers' self-efficacy and professional collaboration	54
Figure 3.9	Teachers' job satisfaction and professional collaboration	55
Figure 4.1	The Community of Learners Network classroom inquiry cycle	69

Executive Summary

What do you need to create a responsive 21st-century school? Three key ingredients are teachers who are confident in their ability to teach, a willingness to innovate, and strong school leaders who establish the conditions in their schools that enable the former two ingredients to flourish. This report, *Schools for 21st-Century Learners: Strong Leaders, Confident Teachers, Innovative Approaches*, uses evidence from the OECD Teaching and Learning International Survey (TALIS), the OECD Programme for International Student Assessment (PISA), and the OECD Innovative Learning Environments project to identify school- and system-level policies that promote effective school leadership, strengthen teacher's sense of self-efficacy, and encourage innovation in creating 21st-century learning environments.

PROMOTING EFFECTIVE SCHOOL LEADERSHIP

Effective school leaders are those who can make evidence-informed decisions, provide the instructional leadership that teachers need to help all their students succeed in school, and create a collaborative school environment in which teachers take part in school decisions. Analysis of TALIS data finds that when teachers participate in decision making in their schools, they report greater confidence in their own ability to teach (self-efficacy). TALIS also finds that school leaders who provide their staff with opportunities to share in decision making tend to report greater job satisfaction.

- **Empower teachers to play a role in decision making at the school level**

  Distributed leadership is not only important to help alleviate some of the burden imposed on school leaders, but it can be beneficial to teachers as well. Policy makers should consider providing guidance on distributed leadership and distributed decision making at the system level.

- **Provide opportunities for, and remove barriers to, continuing professional development for principals**

  In many countries, large proportions of principals reported that there were no relevant opportunities available for professional development and no incentives to participate. Many principals said their work schedules conflicted with opportunities to develop their professional skills. Countries should set standards for high-quality professional learning, aligned with the country's long-term education goals, and ensure that principals can participate in these learning opportunities. In turn, principals must take advantage of the opportunities available to them.

- **Ensure that principals receive training in, and have opportunities to assume, instructional leadership**

  Instructional leadership – focusing on the teaching and learning that take place in school – may be the most important of all principals' tasks. TALIS data show that when principals reported higher levels of instructional leadership, they were also more likely to develop a professional-development plan for their school, observe teaching in the classroom as part of a teacher's formal appraisal, and report there is high level of mutual respect among colleagues at the school. While more training in instructional leadership is needed, principals also need to be made aware of its importance and be offered this training during their initial principal training.

STRENGTHENING TEACHERS' CONFIDENCE IN THEIR OWN ABILITIES

In all countries/economies that participated in TALIS, teachers who reported that they are given opportunities to participate in decision making at school also reported greater job satisfaction and, in most countries, greater self-efficacy. Teachers in nearly all countries who reported that they participate in collaborative professional learning activities five times a year or more also reported significantly higher levels of self-efficacy.

- **Build teachers' capacity to provide instruction for all types of learners**

  Those teachers who reported spending more time keeping order in the classroom also reported less self-efficacy. Initial teacher education should include sufficiently long periods for teachers to practice in a variety of schools. More flexible classroom situations, such as team teaching, might also allow teachers to share the tasks of teaching and disciplining students.

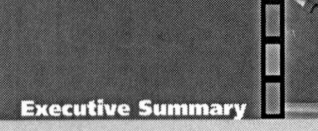

- **Support the development of interpersonal relationships within the school**
  Positive interpersonal relationships with the school leader, other teachers, and students can mitigate the otherwise detrimental effects that challenging classrooms might have on a teacher's satisfaction with his or her job or feelings of self-efficacy. School leaders can provide a physical space in which teachers can meet with each other, or time away from class or other administrative work to allow teachers to meet and develop relationships with students and colleagues. Government policies can give school leaders the organisational freedom to make changes in the school day or school building to help. Teachers need to be open and willing to engage with their colleagues, their administration and their students.

- **Encourage collaboration among teachers**
  It is clear from TALIS data that teachers benefit from even minimal amounts of collaboration with colleagues. Collaborative practices, such as observing other teachers' classes and providing feedback, or teaching as a team in the same class, could – and should – be introduced at school. School leaders could make schedules more flexible to allow for team teaching.

INNOVATING TO CREATE 21ST-CENTURY LEARNING ENVIRONMENTS

Some schools are responding to 21st-century learning needs by regrouping teachers, regrouping learners, rescheduling learning and changing pedagogical approaches.

- **Collaborate and communicate**
  The mere presence of technology in the classroom, in the form of computers or tablets in a school or in mobile phones in the pockets of learners, is not sufficient to foster true innovation in the classroom. All education stakeholders should join together so that the drive to innovate in education is felt throughout the education system, not only in isolated areas. Teachers can play a crucial role as catalysts for change. Wider partnerships and connections should also be constructed, particularly when resources are scarce.

- **Create conditions conducive to innovation**
  Information about the learning taking place in school should be fed back to the various education stakeholders, and incorporated into revised strategies for learning and further innovation. This means that processes for self-evaluation should be in place and that the knowledge base should be developed continually through meaningful research that engages the worlds of policy and practice.

- **Ensure coherence**
  Learning-focused networks and communities of practice should be supported, and coherence with overarching education strategies should be ensured. Ministries and country-level education agencies should provide the legitimacy and the system-wide perspective to push innovation. Ideally, leadership from the local level, from networks and partnerships, and from education authorities at central and local levels should all be working together to create responsive 21st-century learning systems.

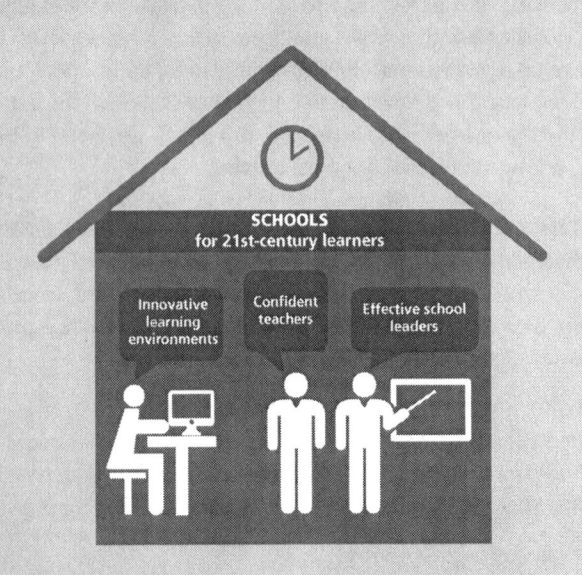

Chapter 1

BUILDING RESPONSIVE SCHOOLS FOR 21ST-CENTURY LEARNERS

Analysis of data from the Teaching and Learning International Survey (TALIS) and the OECD Programme for International Student Assessment (PISA) finds that successful education systems are those that promote leadership at all levels, thereby encouraging teachers and principals, regardless of the formal positions they occupy, to lead innovation in the classroom, the school and the system as a whole. This chapter introduces the three main themes of the 2015 International Summit on the Teaching Profession: leadership, teachers' self-efficacy, and innovation.

Chapter 1

Building responsive schools for 21st-century learners

Globalisation and modernisation are imposing huge changes on individuals and societies. While education is recognised as the key to social and economic progress, across OECD countries, almost one in five 15-year-olds does not acquire a minimum level of skills to be able to contribute meaningfully to society, according to results from PISA 2012, and roughly the same proportion of students drops out of school before they complete their secondary education. In addition, disadvantaged students are twice as likely as their advantaged peers to be poor performers, implying that personal or social circumstances prevent them from realising their potential.

As the 2012 Survey of Adult Skills, a product of the Programme for the International Assessment of Adult Competencies (PIAAC), found, having poor skills in literacy and numeracy severely limits people's access to better-paying and more rewarding jobs. By contrast, among the countries with the largest expansion of university-level education over the past few decades, most still see rising earnings differentials for tertiary graduates, which suggests that the increase in the number of "knowledge workers" has not led to a decrease in their pay, as was the case for low-skilled workers. According to data from the survey, highly skilled individuals are also more likely to volunteer, to see themselves as actors, rather than objects, in the political process, to report good health, and to trust others. Providing all individuals with the knowledge and skills to participate fully in our societies is now a policy imperative.

All this has profound implications for teachers and for the leadership of schools and education systems. The most advanced education systems set ambitious goals for all of their students. They also equip their teachers with the pedagogic skills that have been proven effective, and with enough autonomy so that teachers can use their creativity in determining how their students learn best.

Successful education systems are those that promote leadership at all levels, encouraging teachers and principals, regardless of the formal positions they occupy, to lead innovation in the classroom, the school and the system as a whole. The 2015 International Summit on the Teaching Profession examines the conditions within schools and education systems that encourage deeper and more collaborative forms of **leadership**. Participants consider such questions as:

- How do high-performing countries promote and establish collaborative leadership at all levels within their education systems?
- What strategies (recruitment and retention, career progression, professional development and ongoing professional learning networks) allow education systems to encourage teachers to assume leadership roles?
- How can individual teachers, their unions, and associations of teachers help to create the conditions that promote and support fellow teachers as leaders?

Teachers' self-efficacy, their belief in their own capacity to make a difference, is a prerequisite for improving professional practice and student outcomes. That is why ministers and union leaders have placed **teacher self-efficacy** at the centre of the agenda of the 2015 International Summit on the Teaching Profession, addressing questions such as:

- What are the public policies related to teachers' career progression, performance appraisal, compensation and professional development that contribute to greater self-efficacy among teachers and better learning outcomes?
- How can governments and the teaching profession work together to build both greater teacher efficacy and greater accountability?
- Which education systems have been most successful in achieving a partnership with the teaching profession in order to improve teacher efficacy and student learning?

It is clearly not sufficient to offer more of the same education. The kinds of skills that are easiest to teach and test are also easiest to automate, digitise and outsource. Success is no longer mainly about what we know – Google knows everything – but about what we can do with what we know. Equally important, today's schools need to prepare students to live and work in a world in which most people will need to collaborate with people whose ideas, perspectives and values are different from their own; a world in which people need to decide how to build trust and sustain collaboration across such differences, often bridging space and time with technology; a world in which individual lives will be affected by issues that transcend national boundaries.

One of the most effective "teachers" is failure: often the result of learning through setbacks, stumbles and mistakes is innovation. Innovation is not only what propels economies, it could also transform the teaching profession.

Building responsive schools for 21st-century learners

The 2015 International Summit on the Teaching Profession tries to identify the ingredients of a successful and sustainable system-wide innovation strategy and to define the role of the teaching profession in leading **innovation**, both inside and outside the classroom. This discussion addresses questions like:

- How can education systems and the governments that are responsible for them overcome risk-aversion so that a culture of innovation can take root?

- What encourages teachers to innovate and what constrains them? How can the capacity of individual teachers, and of the teaching profession, to drive innovation be supported? What is the role of new information and communications technology in this regard?

- How do systems and actors, including government officials and teachers' unions, encourage individual innovative teachers and teaching practices as they try to develop an innovative teaching profession?

This publication presents key evidence from the OECD Teaching and Learning International Survey (TALIS) and the OECD Innovative Learning Environments studies that underpins the summit. TALIS is the largest international survey of teachers (see Box 1.1). Launched in 2008, TALIS gives teachers and school leaders (whose roles are not mutually exclusive) around the world a voice to speak about their experiences. The survey focuses on some of the factors that can influence effective teaching. Teachers report on their initial training and professional development activities, the feedback they receive on their teaching, the climate in their classrooms and schools, their satisfaction with their jobs, and their feelings about their professional abilities.

The OECD Innovative Learning Environments (ILE) project analyses how young people learn. It studies the conditions and dynamics that are most conducive to learning. By identifying concrete examples of innovative learning environments from all over the world, ILE aims to inform practice, leadership and reform.

Figures and tables that are cited, but not included, in this report are taken from *TALIS 2013 Results: An International Perspective on Teaching and Learning* (OECD, 2014), *Innovative Learning Environments* (OECD, 2013a) and *PISA 2012 Results* (OECD, 2013b, 2013c, 2013d, 2013e, 2013f) unless otherwise indicated.

Box 1.1. The TALIS Design

International target population: Lower secondary education teachers and leaders of mainstream schools.

Target sample size: 200 schools per country; 20 teachers and 1 school leader in each school.

School samples: Representative samples of schools and teachers within schools.

Target response rates: 75% of the sampled schools, together with a 75% response rate from all sampled teachers in the country. A school is considered to have responded if 50% of sampled teachers respond.

Questionnaires: Separate questionnaires for teachers and school leaders, each requiring between 45 and 60 minutes to complete.

Mode of data collection: Questionnaires filled in on paper or on line.

Survey windows: September-December 2012 for Southern Hemisphere countries and February-June 2013 for Northern Hemisphere countries.

Source: OECD (2014), *TALIS 2013 Results: An International Perspective on Teaching and Learning*, http://dx.doi.org/10.1787/9789264196261-en.

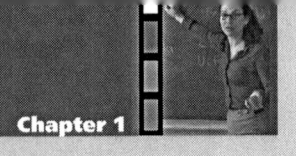

References

OECD (2014), *TALIS 2013 Results: An International Perspective on Teaching and Learning*, OECD Publishing, Paris, http://dx.doi.org/10.1787/9789264196261-en.

OECD (2013a), *Innovative Learning Environments*, Educational Research and Innovation, OECD Publishing, Paris, http://dx.doi.org/10.1787/9789264203488-en.

OECD (2013b), *PISA 2012 Results: What Students Know and Can Do (Volume I, Revised edition, February 2014): Student Performance in Mathematics, Reading and Science*, PISA, OECD Publishing, http://dx.doi.org/10.1787/9789264208780-en.

OECD (2013c), *PISA 2012 Results: Excellence through Equity (Volume II): Giving Every Student the Chance to Succeed*, PISA, OECD Publishing, Paris, http://dx.doi.org/10.1787/9789264201132-en.

OECD (2013d), *PISA 2012 Results: Ready to Learn (Volume III): Students' Engagement, Drive and Self-Beliefs*, PISA, OECD Publishing, Paris, http://dx.doi.org/10.1787/9789264201170-en.

OECD (2013e), *PISA 2012 Results: What Makes Schools Successful (Volume IV): Resources, Policies and Practices*, PISA, OECD Publishing, Paris, http://dx.doi.org/10.1787/9789264201156-en.

OECD (2013f), *PISA 2012 Results: Creative Problem Solving (Volume V): Students' Skills in Tackling Real-Life Problems*, PISA, OECD Publishing, Paris, http://dx.doi.org/10.1787/9789264208070-en.

Chapter 2
PROMOTING EFFECTIVE SCHOOL LEADERSHIP

This chapter discusses the roles and responsibilities of school leaders. Based on data from the 2013 Teaching and Learning International Survey (TALIS), it presents a profile of today's school principals: their background and education, and the professional tasks they find the most rewarding. The chapter also examines the importance of sharing leadership responsibilities (distributed leadership) and providing guidance to teachers (instructional leadership).

Chapter 2
Promoting effective school leadership

The OECD Programme for International Student Assessment (PISA) shows that a substantial proportion of students in OECD countries now attends schools that are highly autonomous in different areas of decision making. PISA also finds that high-performing and equitable school systems tend to grant greater autonomy to schools in formulating and using curricula and assessments. In some countries, the main expression of school autonomy is when schools develop and adapt curricula. In others, autonomy is manifested in the management and administration of individual schools, even while, in some cases, education systems are moving towards more centralised governance of curricula and standards. Beyond questions of autonomy, many schools are confronted with increasing social diversity in the classroom, students with special needs, high dropout rates, and relatively large proportions of students who leave school without the basic knowledge and skills necessary to be able to participate in an increasingly competitive global economy.

What schools need to meet these challenges are effective leaders who can make evidence-informed decisions, provide the instructional leadership that teachers need to help all their students succeed in school, and create a collaborative school environment in which teachers take part in school decisions. Analysis of TALIS data finds that in-school relations have a significant impact on teachers' self-efficacy (their confidence in their own ability to teach) and job satisfaction. In 20 countries, teachers who agreed that the staff at their school is provided with opportunities to participate in decision making reported higher self-efficacy scores (OECD, 2014, Table 7.8). An even more uniform and strong relationship is observed with job satisfaction. The ability to participate in decision making at school is significantly related to a strong improvement in teachers' job satisfaction across all countries (OECD, 2014, Table 7.9).

There are four take-away points from the analyses of TALIS data. First, in-school relations are important for teachers' self-efficacy and job satisfaction. Second, school leaders should try to focus on encouraging collaborative relationships among teachers and positive relationships between teachers and students in their schools. Third, school leaders who work to provide school staff with opportunities to share in decision making may gain returns in the realm of higher job satisfaction. And fourth, there is little evidence that instructional leadership is associated with higher self-efficacy or job satisfaction among teachers.

Box 2.1. Promoting teacher leadership in the United States

Teach to Lead is an effort co-led by the U.S. Department of Education and the National Board for Professional Teaching Standards. Speaking at the annual Teaching and Learning conference in March 2014, U.S. Secretary of Education Arne Duncan announced the initiative, aimed at advancing student outcomes by expanding opportunities for teacher leadership – particularly those that allow teachers to stay in the classroom and in the profession they love.

Since December 2014, Teach to Lead has held a series of regional Teacher Leadership Summits to spotlight and advance innovative, teacher-led work in states, districts and schools. The goal of the summits is to bring together educators from across the country to spur meaningful advances in teacher leadership. Educators submitted proposals via Commit to Lead, the online community of Teach to Lead. The proposals could entail scaling existing programmes, creating new programmes or spearheading supportive policies that give teachers more opportunities to lead, particularly while continuing to teach. In these working meetings, participants and supporter organisations (including the Hope Street Group, the National Network of State Teachers of the Year and Teach Plus) have shared resources and collaborated to create action plans in order to realise their leadership ideas. In addition to the summits, Commit to Lead is designed to allow educators to share and collaborate on promising ideas that advance teacher leadership and address pressing problems in education.

Secretary Duncan will report back on the year's work and next steps at the 2015 Teaching and Learning Summit in March.

Source: U.S. Department of Education.

TALIS 2018 provides a wealth of information about the role of principals as school leaders. It also provides some data about the extent to which leadership is distributed in schools, and teachers are given the opportunity to participate in school decisions. However, much of the analysis from TALIS, to date, has focused on principals, which is reflected in this chapter.

The TALIS 2013 survey found that:

- Principals in countries and economies that participated in TALIS have a demanding set of responsibilities. On average, principals spend 41% of their time managing human and material resources, planning, reporting and adhering to regulations.

- In some countries, principals who show high levels of instructional leadership are more likely to report that they use student performance and student evaluation results to develop the school's education goals and programmes, and to report that they have a professional development plan for their school.

- Principals who provide more instructional leadership tend to spend more time on curriculum and teaching-related tasks; in most countries they are more likely to directly observe classroom teaching as part of the formal appraisal of teachers' work.

- Principals who report that leadership is well distributed and who frequently provide instructional leadership also report greater job satisfaction; by contrast, principals who report heavier workloads and a lack of shared work and decision making report less job satisfaction.

- On average across TALIS-participating countries and economies, school principals have 21 years of teaching experience.

- Principals across the countries and economies that participated in TALIS are well educated. Most have completed formal education at the tertiary level, including programmes in school administration, principal training, teacher preparation and/or instructional leadership.

WHAT SCHOOL PRINCIPALS DO

A strong school leader establishes a climate conducive to teaching and learning and fosters community support for the efforts of the teaching staff. In many countries, concern about improving student achievement results has made strong school leadership a priority (Pont et al., 2008; Branch et al., 2013). The literature devoted to principal leadership is replete with examples of the ways that principals exert leadership, including: defining the school's goals and programme (Grissom et al., 2013) and its professional development plan (OECD, 2013); collaborating with teachers to solve classroom discipline problems (MacNeil and Prater, 1999); observing instruction (Veenman et al., 1998); encouraging teachers to take responsibility for improving their teaching and for student learning; and providing parents or guardians with information about the school and about student performance (Jeynes, 2011).

Figure 2.1
Principals' working time
Average proportion of time lower secondary education principals report spending on the following activities

- Administrative and leadership tasks and meetings
- Curriculum and teaching-related tasks and meetings
- Student interactions
- Interactions with parents or guardians
- Interactions with local and regional community, business and industry
- Other

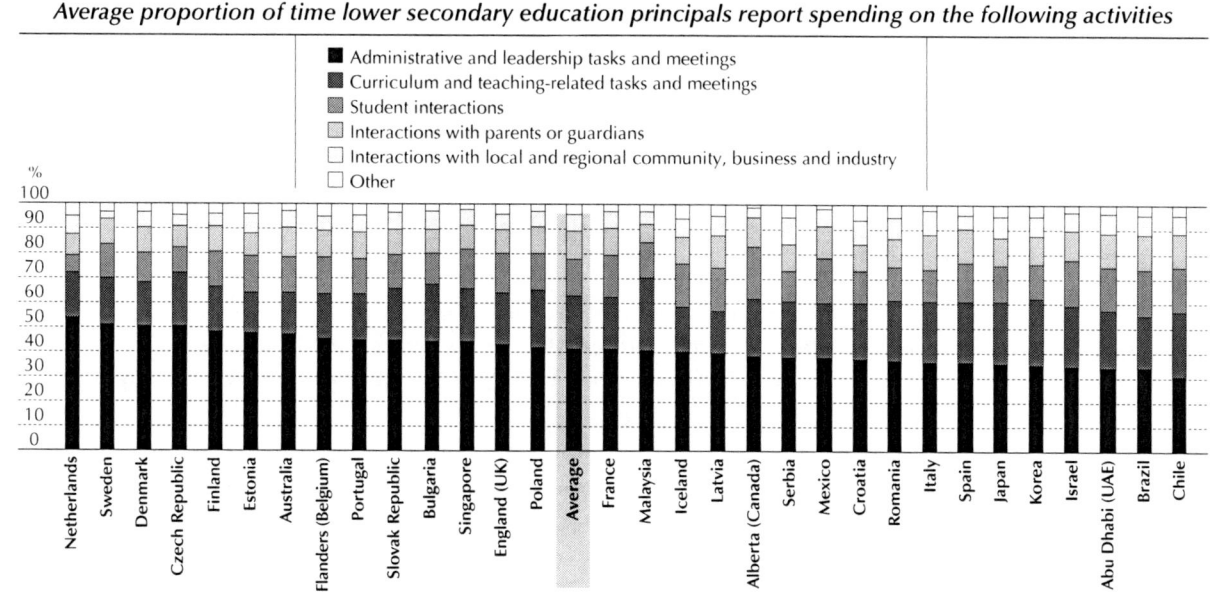

Countries are ranked in descending order, based on the percentage of time principals spend on administrative and leadership tasks and meetings.
Source: OECD, TALIS 2013 Database, Table 3.1.
StatLink http://dx.doi.org/10.1787/888933041231

Chapter 2
Promoting effective school leadership

School principals who participated in the TALIS 2013 survey were asked how they distribute their work time. As Figure 2.1 indicates, on average, principals reported that they devote 41% of their time to administrative and leadership tasks and meetings; 21% of their time to curriculum and teaching-related tasks and meetings; 15% to interactions with students; 11% to interactions with parents or guardians; and 7% to interactions with local and regional community, businesses and industries (OECD, 2014, Table 3.1). While the time spent on each of these tasks varies considerably among countries, Figure 2.1 shows that nearly two-thirds of principals' time, on average, is spent on administrative and leadership tasks and on curriculum and teaching-related tasks and meetings. While this can be seen as the main business of the school and main responsibility for principals, it leaves very little time for principals to carry out other tasks.

The TALIS survey asked principals about the leadership activities in which they were engaged during the preceding 12 months. Figure 2.2 presents data about the proportion of principals who reported that they engaged "frequently" in specific leadership activities.[1]

Figure 2.2
Principals' leadership

Percentage of lower secondary education principals who report having engaged in the following leadership activities, and the frequency in which they engaged, during the 12 months prior to the survey

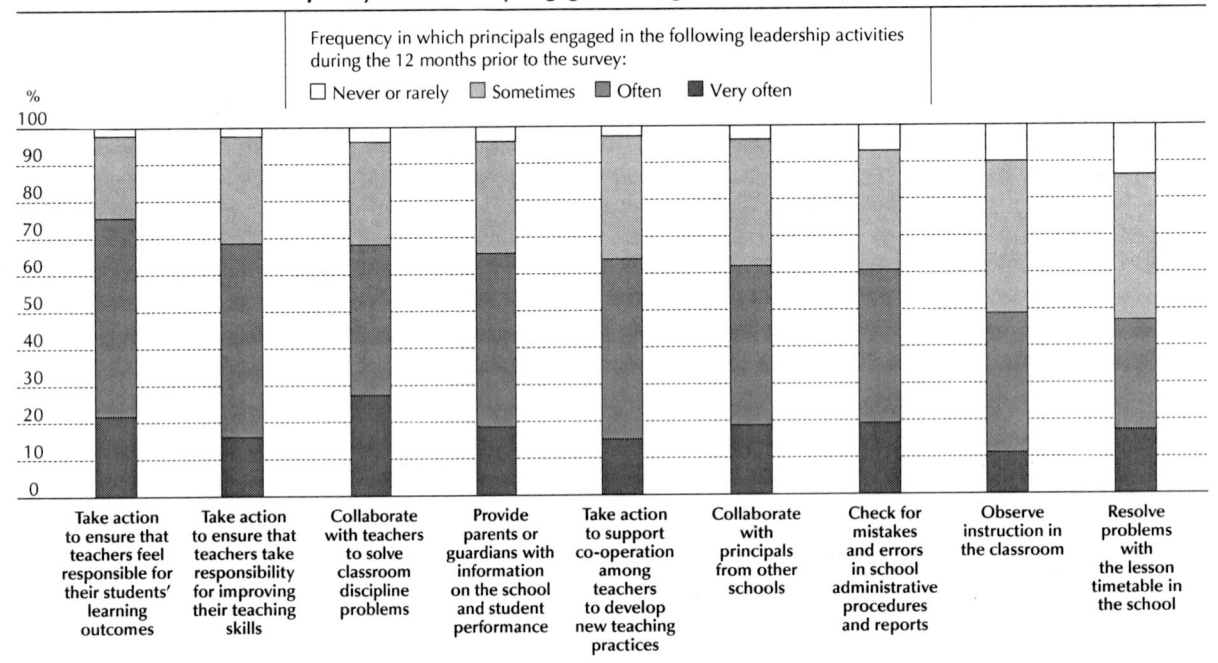

Leadership activities are ranked in descending order, based on the percentage of principals who engaged "often" or "very often" in a specific leadership activity during the 12 months prior to the survey.
Source: OECD, TALIS 2013 Database, Tables 3.2 and 3.2.Web.
StatLink http://dx.doi.org/10.1787/888933041250

Among the most challenging of a teacher's responsibilities is maintaining a productive and orderly environment in which he or she can teach and students can learn (see, for example, MacNeil and Prater, 1999). Students cannot learn and teachers cannot teach if students are unruly. In fact, results from PISA show that classroom climate is closely related to student learning outcomes.

Collaboration between principals and teachers to solve classroom discipline problems varies significantly across countries. Malaysia and Romania are on one end of the spectrum: in these countries, more than 90% of principals reported frequent collaboration with teachers to solve disciplinary problems. Australia, Estonia, Iceland, Japan, the Netherlands and England (United Kingdom) are at the other end of the spectrum, where more than half of principals (58%-72%) reported infrequent collaboration with teachers to solve classroom discipline problems (OECD, 2014, Table 3.2). The patterns reported here may reflect differences in disciplinary issues among countries rather than differences in the degree to which principals focus on disciplinary matters.

© OECD 2015 SCHOOLS FOR 21ST-CENTURY LEARNERS: STRONG LEADERS, CONFIDENT TEACHERS, INNOVATIVE APPROACHES

In addition to the help principals may provide in solving disciplinary problems in the classroom, principals observe instruction and give teachers feedback based on their observations. On average, nearly half (49%) of school leaders reported that they frequently observe instruction in the classroom. Based on evidence from a programme for training Dutch principals in coaching skills, Veenman et al. (1998) show, among other things, that principal coaching helped to strengthen teacher autonomy, enabling teachers to assess the effectiveness of their own teaching and to formulate plans for improving it. The result of better teaching is better student learning.

Teachers must also keep their knowledge and practice up to date. By encouraging teachers to learn from one another, principals help teachers to remain current in their practice and to develop more collaborative practices with their colleagues at school. Principals were asked about taking action to encourage co-operation among teachers to develop new teaching practices. As Figure 2.2 indicates, 64% of principals reported taking such action frequently (ranging from 34% in Japan to 98% in Malaysia), on average (see also Table 3.2.Web). The largest proportions of principals (between 80% and 98%) who reported that they frequently encourage such co-operation among their teachers are observed in Chile, Malaysia, Romania, Serbia, the Slovak Republic and Abu Dhabi (United Arab Emirates). By contrast, in Denmark, Estonia, Japan, the Netherlands and Flanders (Belgium), more than half of principals reported that they never, rarely or only sometimes encourage such co-operation. It would be interesting to learn whether this is simply a lack of action on the part of principals in these countries or whether such action is simply unnecessary because teachers in these schools already enjoy a culture of co-operation.

Students' achievement depends on the experience and skills of their teachers (Jepsen and Rivkin, 2009; Huang and Moon, 2009; Biniaminov and Glasman, 1983; Veldman and Brophy, 1974). Principals can play an important part in ensuring that teachers assume responsibility for improving their teaching skills. Figure 2.2 shows that, on average, most principals (69%) do so (OECD, 2014, Table 3.2). This proportion ranges from 39% in Japan to 95% in Malaysia. The largest proportions are found in Bulgaria (88%), Chile (88%), Malaysia (95%), Romania (85%), Serbia (82%), Singapore (84%) and Abu Dhabi (United Arab Emirates) (93%). More than half of principals in Finland (60%), Japan (61%), Norway (53%), Sweden (56%) and Flanders (Belgium) (59%) reported that they never, rarely or only sometimes ensure that teachers assume responsibility for improving their teaching skills.

Many principals also remind teachers about the importance of taking responsibility for what their students learn. On average, 76% of principals (ranging from 33% in Japan to 100% in Malaysia) reported they frequently take such action (OECD, 2014, Table 3.2).

Student success is enhanced when teachers' efforts are complemented by support from parents (Jeynes, 2011). Parents play an important role in supporting the school and the success of their children; but to do so effectively, they must have accurate information from and about the school. The responsibility for providing parents or guardians with information about the school and student performance sometimes rests with the principal. As seen in Figure 2.2, two-thirds of principals, on average, reported that they provide this information frequently.

Identifying and correcting errors in administrative procedures or reports and resolving problems with the school's schedule of lessons are two of the many administrative tasks that principals perform. On average, 61% of principals said that they check frequently for mistakes and errors in school administrative procedures and reports. On average, slightly less than half of principals (47%) said that they frequently resolve problems with the lesson schedule in the school. Both of these administrative tasks are important, yet in some countries principals are freed from this administrative burden. It would be interesting to learn how and whether these tasks are distributed to other members of the school staff in these countries.

Principals can learn from and support one another through collaboration. On average, 62% of principals reported that they frequently collaborate with their peers in other schools (OECD, 2014, Table 3.2). Large proportions of principals in Finland (82%), Malaysia (89%), the Netherlands (86%), Romania (87%) and Serbia (96%) reported that they frequently collaborate with principals from other schools. In contrast, significant proportions of principals in Brazil (10%), Chile (18%), Israel (8%) and Spain (9%) reported that they never or rarely collaborate with principals in other schools.

SHARING RESPONSIBILITIES

Principals are increasingly responsible for such disparate tasks as appointing, hiring, suspending and dismissing teachers; determining the allocation of school resources; approving student admission; establishing the school's disciplinary and assessment policies; and determining which courses the school offers, course content, and instructional resources.

Precisely because principals' work has become so complex, some of these responsibilities should be more broadly shared with others, both inside and outside the school (Schleicher, 2012). And as TALIS shows, teachers tend to report a greater sense of self-efficacy and more job satisfaction when they are given the opportunity to participate in decision making at school.

TALIS calculates the percentage of principals who have significant responsibility for such tasks and who also reported that they share some of these responsibilities with others (OECD, 2014, Table 3.4). When a principal reports that the responsibility for a task is shared, this means that the principal and other members of the school management team, teachers who are not part of the school management team, a school's governing board, or a local or national authority participate in decision making.

The data reveal a wide variation among countries in the extent to which principals share responsibility for various tasks (OECD, 2014, Table 3.4). For example, 75% of principals or more in Croatia, Denmark, and the Netherlands reported that they share responsibility for appointing teachers while 20% of principals or less in Bulgaria, France, Japan, Korea, Malaysia and Mexico so reported (the average across countries is 39%). More than half of the principals in Croatia, Denmark, the Netherlands, Serbia and England (United Kingdom) reported that they share responsibility for dismissing or suspending teachers from employment; but in Bulgaria, the Czech Republic, France, Japan, Korea, Malaysia, Mexico, Poland, Spain and Sweden, 20% of principals or less so reported (the average across countries is 29%). Far smaller proportions of principals reported that they share responsibility for establishing teachers' salaries and pay scales (14% on average) or for determining teachers' salary increases (18% on average). Only in Latvia and England (United Kingdom) did more than half of principals indicate that they share responsibility for establishing teachers' salaries and pay scales. Similarly, only in Estonia, Latvia and England (United Kingdom) did more than half of principals report that they share responsibility for determining salary increases for teachers.

On average, nearly half of principals (47%) reported that they share responsibility for deciding on budget allocations within the school. In Chile, Korea, Mexico, Romania and Abu Dhabi (United Arab Emirates), however, fewer than one in four principals reported this. In contrast, more than three in four principals in Denmark and Latvia reported that they share this responsibility.

In general, the majority of principals reported sharing responsibility with regard to managing student discipline policies (61% on average) and assessment policies (52% on average). Many principals reported sharing responsibility for tasks related to choosing which learning materials are used (45%), determining course content (35%) and deciding which courses are offered (52%).

The variations in the extent to which particular responsibilities are shared are likely to reflect both the policy contexts in which principals work and principals' individual decisions about how they delegate responsibility. Schools may have autonomy in some areas but not in others. For example, teachers may be appointed by principals in some contexts, but salaries and salary increases may be determined by collective agreements negotiated outside the local school.

More than one in three principals (37%) reported sharing responsibility for approving students for admission to the school. This is especially common in the Netherlands, where more than 80% of principals reported so, while less than 20% of principals in Japan, Korea, Malaysia, Poland and Sweden did.

Distributed leadership

In addition to looking at the tasks that a principal may or may not share with colleagues, TALIS 2013 also asked principals about whether there was a collaborative culture in the school for making decisions. When school decisions involve not only the principal but others in the school who do not occupy the formal post of principal, including other members of the school's management team, vice-principals, and classroom teachers, this can be referred to as *distributed leadership* or *distributed decision making* (see, for example, Harris, 2008; Harris, 2012; Leithwood et al., 2009; Smylie et al., 2007).

Figure 2.3 shows how principals responded to statements that describe the collaborative culture in their schools (some of which were used to create an index of distributed leadership; see Box 2.2 below). On average across the countries and economies that participated in TALIS, more than nine in ten principals agreed that there is a collaborative culture in their schools, which is characterised by mutual support, or that the school provides staff with opportunities to participate in decision making. Along the same lines, only about one in three principals agreed that they make important decisions on their own. This would indicate that, according to school leaders, most schools in TALIS-participating countries and economies enjoy some level of distributed leadership for decision making.

Promoting effective school leadership

Figure 2.3
School decisions and collaborative school culture

Percentage of lower secondary education principals who "strongly disagree", "disagree", "agree" or "strongly agree" with the following statement about their school

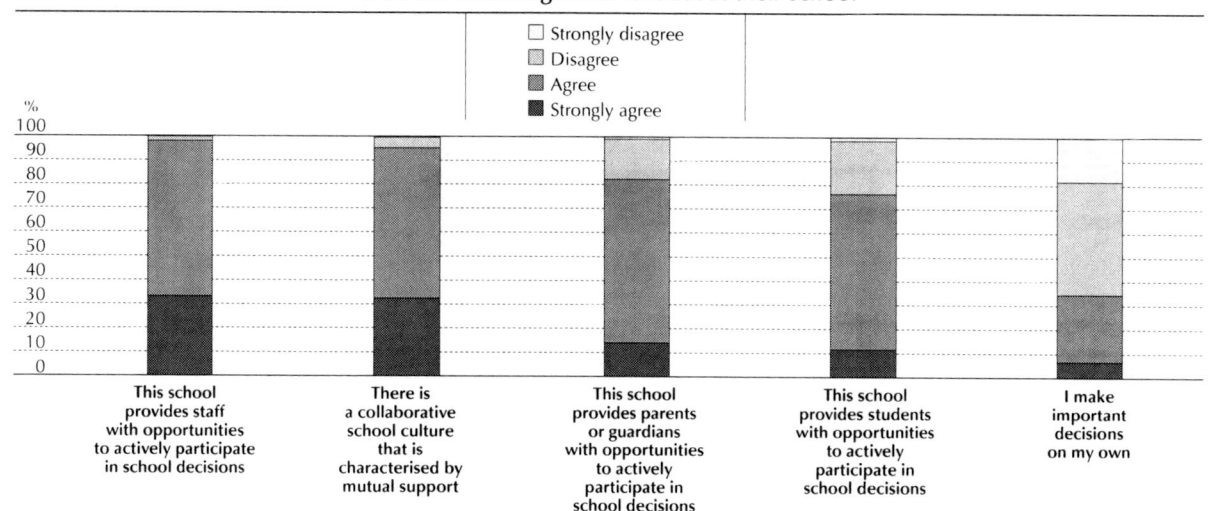

[Bar chart with categories: Strongly disagree, Disagree, Agree, Strongly agree]

Categories (left to right):
- This school provides staff with opportunities to actively participate in school decisions
- There is a collaborative school culture that is characterised by mutual support
- This school provides parents or guardians with opportunities to actively participate in school decisions
- This school provides students with opportunities to actively participate in school decisions
- I make important decisions on my own

Items are ranked in descending order, based on the percentage of principals who "agree" or "strongly agree" with the statement about their school.
Source: OECD, TALIS 2013 Database, Table 3.35. Web.
StatLink http://dx.doi.org/10.1787/888933041288

Box 2.2. Description of the principal distributed leadership index

To measure distributed leadership, TALIS asked principals how strongly they agreed or disagreed with these statements regarding decision-making responsibilities at their school:

- This school provides staff with opportunities to actively participate in school decisions.
- This school provides parents or guardians with opportunities to actively participate in school decisions.
- This school provides students with opportunities to actively participate in school decisions.

Source: OECD (2014), *TALIS 2013 Results: An International Perspective on Teaching and Learning*, http://dx.doi.org/10.1787/9789264196261-en.

TALIS finds a consistent relationship between distributed leadership and school climate. Principals in 23 countries reported using more distributed leadership when working in schools with a positive school climate, characterised by mutual respect, openness and sharing among colleagues (OECD, 2014, Table 3.7). Sharing decision-making responsibilities might be easier in such a climate or, conversely, might help to develop such a school climate; TALIS data do not suggest the direction of the relationship. Moreover, in just over half (17) of TALIS countries, principals who reported more distributed leadership also tended to report greater job satisfaction (OECD, 2014, Table 3.19). If governments – and school principals themselves – want to see greater job satisfaction among principals, then they might encourage more distribution of leadership in schools.

The TALIS data confirm that the job of principal encompasses a wide range of complex tasks and responsibilities. When comparing the data across countries, the extent of principals' participation in various administrative and leadership activities is found to differ significantly, either by choice, circumstance or authority. However, most principals in all countries work to develop their school's education goals and programmes; in some countries, virtually all principals do. A smaller proportion – but still sizable in many countries – works to prepare their schools' professional development plans. Principals are aided in both of these endeavours by the increasing availability of student performance and evaluation data. The extent to which principals share responsibility for tasks or decisions also varies by country as well as by the nature of the specific task or decision. TALIS data could be used to support the development of standards for the profession and to help identify the kinds of initial training or professional development activities that might be required for prospective and current principals.

Chapter 2 Promoting effective school leadership

DEFINING SCHOOL GOALS, PROGRAMMES AND PROFESSIONAL DEVELOPMENT PLANS

With greater availability of and access to data concerning schools' and students' performance come growing demands for accountability (Vanhoof et al., 2014). Today, more than at any time in the past, principals are responsible for developing their school's education goals and programmes, and for using student performance and results of student evaluations to develop those goals and programmes.

Data about principals' participation in activities related to school development plans appear in Figure 2.4 (OECD, 2014, Table 3.3). Nearly nine in ten principals, on average across TALIS-participating countries and economies, reported using student performance and student evaluation results, including national or international assessments, to develop the school's education goals and programmes.

In addition to developing their school's goals and programmes, principals are increasingly responsible for establishing a professional development plan for their school. Although developing this plan is an important facet of a principal's work, the proportion of principals who reported that they work on such a plan (79%) is nearly 10 percentage points smaller, on average, than the proportion of principals who reported that they use student performance and student evaluation results to develop their school's education goals and programmes. Figure 2.4 shows that this pattern is found in most countries.

Figure 2.4
Principals' participation in a school development plan
Percentage of lower secondary education principals who report having engaged in the following activities related to a school development plan in the 12 months prior to the survey

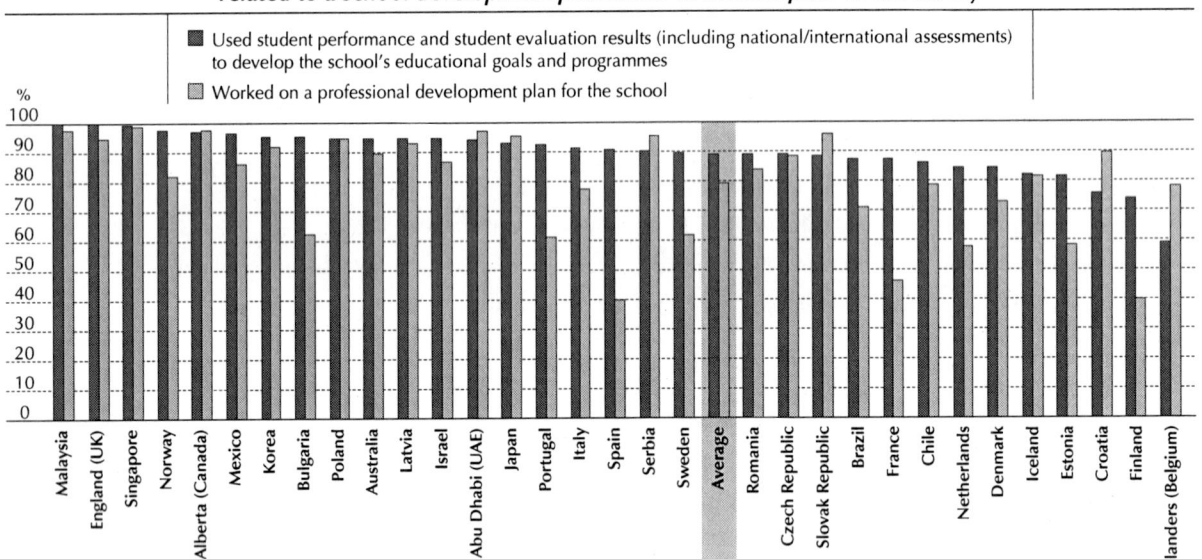

- Used student performance and student evaluation results (including national/international assessments) to develop the school's educational goals and programmes
- Worked on a professional development plan for the school

Countries are ranked in descending order, based on the percentage of principals who used student performance and student evaluation results (including national/international assessments) to develop the school's educational goals and programmes.
Source: OECD, TALIS 2013 Database, Table 3.3.
StatLink http://dx.doi.org/10.1787/888933041269

PROVIDING DIRECTION TO THE SCHOOL AND SUPPORTING TEACHERS: INSTRUCTIONAL LEADERSHIP

Schools have multiple responsibilities, the most important of which is to equip students with the knowledge and dispositions they need to assume the responsibilities that come with adult citizenship. Improving student achievement, while always an important goal of schooling, has become more prominent as adults are now required to compete in a global economy. Instructional leadership is evident in much of the work that principals do, including ensuring that the goals of the school are well articulated, that the school's environment is one that is safe and conducive to learning, and that teachers' efforts are focused on instruction and on improving their own practice. Box 2.3 discusses how instructional leadership is measured in TALIS.

> **Box 2.3. Description of the instructional leadership index**
>
> To measure instructional leadership, TALIS asked principals to indicate how frequently they engaged in the following activities in their school during the 12 months prior to the survey. Response options ranged from "never or rarely" to "very often".
> - I took actions to support co-operation among teachers to develop new teaching practices.
> - I took actions to ensure that teachers take responsibility for improving their teaching skills.
> - I took actions to ensure that teachers feel responsible for their students' learning outcomes.
>
> **Source:** OECD (2014), *TALIS 2013 Results: An International Perspective on Teaching and Learning,* http://dx.doi.org/10.1787/9789264196261-en.

Principals are required to provide direction for the school and ensure that teachers' appraisals give teachers the tools with which they can be effective teachers. Principals can fulfil these responsibilities in part by using student performance and evaluation results to develop education goals and programmes and by working on a professional development plan for the school. The former is about establishing the school's focus and aligning its programme with those goals; the latter is concerned with ensuring that the school's staff has the capacity to reach the goals by implementing the school's programmes.

Principals can also ensure that the outcomes of teacher appraisals are meaningful. In six countries, principals who reported high levels of instructional leadership tended to be more likely to report that they use student performance and student evaluation results to develop the school's education goals and programmes (OECD, 2014, Table 3.16). Similarly, in 13 countries, principals who reported higher levels of instructional leadership are more likely to have reported that they are working on a professional development plan for their school. In addition, in Australia, Denmark, Israel, the Netherlands, Sweden and Flanders [Belgium], principals who reported higher levels of instructional leadership tended to report that they spend more time on curriculum and teaching-related tasks (OECD, 2014, Table 3.17). And in 20 countries, principals who reported higher levels of instructional leadership were more likely to report that they directly observe classroom teaching as part of the formal appraisal of teachers' work (OECD, 2014, Table 3.16). What this shows is that principals who reported higher levels of instructional leadership also reported that they spend more time on tasks directly related to teaching, learning and the development of their teachers' practices.

TALIS data also indicate that instructional leadership is related to some of the actions taken following teacher appraisal. Principals have a range of actions they can take following an appraisal of a teacher's performance, including developing a plan for improvement, appointing a mentor or imposing negative sanctions.

In nine countries, principals who reported higher levels of instructional leadership more frequently reported that a development or training plan is created for teachers following an appraisal (OECD, 2014, Table 3.16). Similarly, in ten countries, the association between instructional leadership and appointing a mentor to help the teacher improve is positive.

Higher levels of instructional leadership do not appear to be related to the likelihood of imposing material sanctions, such as reducing a teacher's salary, after teacher appraisals. In only five countries is instructional leadership related to the likelihood of making a change in a teacher's work responsibilities after the teacher is appraised (OECD, 2014, Table 3.16).

In six countries, higher levels of instructional leadership are associated with changes in the likelihood of a teacher's career advancement after the teacher is appraised. Only in Bulgaria, Malaysia and Spain is the dismissal of a teacher or non-renewal of a contract following a teacher appraisal more likely to be reported by principals who also reported higher levels of instructional leadership; the reverse is observed in Chile (OECD, 2014, Table 3.16).

Instructional leadership and school climate

In most countries and economies that participated in TALIS, the majority of teachers work in environments with a positive professional climate. Data from the principal questionnaire indicate that principals share this feeling of a positive climate. TALIS examines the relationship between instructional leadership and principals' reports on the factors that contribute to school climate, such as shortages of school resources (materials and personnel), delinquency in the school, the degree of mutual respect, and the proportion of administrative and support staff in the school (OECD, 2014, Table 3.18).

In 17 countries, principals who reported higher levels of instructional leadership tended to report that they work in schools that have more positive school climates, characterised by high levels of mutual respect. As was noted earlier, this could mean either that the climate of mutual respect already existing in a school makes instructional leadership easier or that the instructional leadership exerted by the principals promotes a climate of mutual respect. Either way, the school benefits. The other school climate variables examined do not appear to have consistent relationships with principals' instructional leadership.

PRINCIPALS' WORK EXPERIENCE

Regardless of the level or type of education that a principal might have attained, there is sometimes no substitute for experience. No amount of formal education can prepare a person for some of the situations that might be encountered in school, and these experiences can shape a principal's behaviour and actions.

Figure 2.5 provides evidence about the work experience that principals bring to their responsibilities (OECD, 2014, Table 3.12). The data indicate that across TALIS-participating countries and economies, school principals have an average of 9 years of experience in the role, ranging from an average of 3 years in Korea to 13 years in Denmark and Latvia. Comparatively large proportions of the principals in Korea (47%) and Portugal (39%) have less than 3 years of experience in the role. Bulgaria, Chile, Estonia and Italy are at the other end of the spectrum, with approximately one in five of their principals having more than 20 years of experience as principal.

Figure 2.5
Work experience of principals

Percentage of lower secondary education principals with the following average years of experience in each role

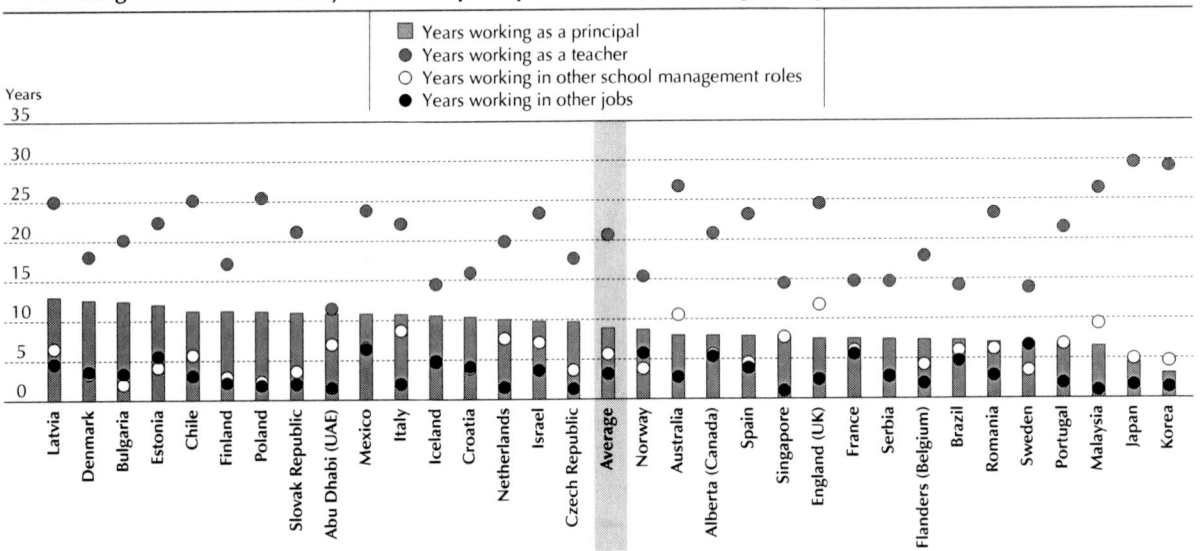

Countries are ranked in descending order, based on the years of working experience as a principal.
Source: OECD, TALIS 2013 Database, Table 3.12.
StatLink http://dx.doi.org/10.1787/888933041364

School principals bring a variety of prior experiences to their roles as principal, including working in other school-management roles, working as teachers and experience in other jobs. On average, lower secondary school principals have spent 6 years in other management roles, ranging from 2 years (Bulgaria and Poland) to 12 years (England [United Kingdom]). TALIS data confirm that experience as a principal is typically built upon a foundation of teaching experience. On average, principals have 21 years of teaching experience.

Leading and teaching are both demanding responsibilities, and principals' teaching obligations vary widely among countries (OECD, 2014, Table 3.13). At one end of the spectrum are nine countries in which more than 90% of principals are employed full time (90% of their time) as principals and have no teaching responsibilities. At the other end are Bulgaria, the Czech Republic, Malaysia, and the Slovak Republic, where 90% or more of full-time principals must balance their work as both principals and teachers. While principals who must also work as teachers have many extra tasks to accomplish, retaining some teaching responsibilities also keeps them closer to the core job of the school.

These principals are able to maintain a different kind of relationship with students – and possibly with the teaching staff – and can even test some of the policies they are trying to enact at the wider school level.

PROFESSIONAL DEVELOPMENT FOR PRINCIPALS

The application of specialised knowledge is one of the hallmarks of professionalism (Goode, 1969; Larson, 1977; Epstein and Hundert, 2002; Gerrard, 2012). School leaders, as professionals, acknowledge their need for further development of their skills and actively engage in such activities. Figure 2.6 provides data about the percentage of principals who participated in a professional network, mentoring or research activity; courses, conferences or observation visits; or other types of professional development activities in the 12 months prior to the survey (OECD, 2014, Table 3.14). On average across the countries and economies that participated in TALIS, principals spent 20 days participating in a professional network, mentoring or research activity; 13 days in courses, conferences or observation visits; and 10 days in other types of professional development activities.

Figure 2.6
Principals' recent professional development

Participation rates and average number of days of professional development reported to be undertaken by lower secondary education principals in the 12 months prior to the survey

	Percentage of principals who participated in the following professional development activities in the 12 months prior to the survey	Average number of days of participation among those who participated
Percentage of principals who participated in courses, conferences or observation visits	83%	13
Percentage of principals who participated in a professional network, mentoring or research activity	51%	20
Percentage of principals who participated in other types of professional development activities	34%	10

Items are ranked in descending order, based on the percentage of principals participating in professional development activities in the 12 months prior to the survey.
Source: OECD, TALIS 2013 Database, Table 3.14.
StatLink http://dx.doi.org/10.1787/888933041383

As a consequence of school-improvement efforts, it is increasingly common for professionals in education to participate in collaborative professional learning activities, where professionals work together to examine their practice and acquire new knowledge (DuFour, 2004). The proportions of principals across TALIS-participating countries and economies who have engaged in professional networks, mentoring or research activities during the 12 months prior to the survey and the average numbers of days spent by those who participated vary considerably. Small proportions of principals in the Czech Republic (28%), Portugal (11%), Romania (29%), Serbia (21%) and Spain (28%) reported that they had participated in a professional network, mentoring or research activity during the preceding 12 months, in contrast to the large proportions of principals in Australia (84%), the Netherlands (87%) and Singapore (93%) who reported the same.

The amount of time spent on these activities varies as well. For example, in 11 countries, principals spent fewer than 10 days on such activities. However, the proportions of principals in these 11 countries who were engaged in these activities – even for a short amount of time – ranged from 42% in Sweden to 84% in Australia.

Australia provides an interesting example of how to develop a standard for the role of principal that takes into account the overarching goals of schooling and the cultural context in which schooling occurs (Box 2.4). Adopting such a standard could, over time, help to elevate the status of the principal and provide guidance on principals' preparation, conduct and professional development.

The percentages of principals who participated in courses, conferences or observation visits ranged from 54% in France to 99% in Singapore. For other types of professional development activities, percentages ranged from 15% in Bulgaria to 58% in Malaysia. The range of the average number of days spent in each activity was modest, from an average of 4 days (France) to 37 days (Brazil) in courses, conferences or observation visits, and from 4 days (Australia, Croatia, Finland, Japan and England [United Kingdom]) to 37 days (Mexico) for other types of professional development activities. While participation in professional development is generally supported for school leaders and teachers alike, spending 37 days away from school each year attending courses or conferences or making observation visits may prove to be excessive, given a principal's busy schedule.

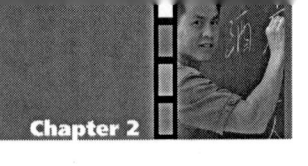

Box 2.4. Australia's approach to school leadership and its National Professional Standard for Principals

The Australian Institute for Teaching and School Leadership was created in 2010 to promote excellence in the teaching and school leadership profession. A public, independent institution supported by the Ministry of Education, its role is to develop and maintain national professional standards for teaching and school leadership, implement an agreed system of national accreditation of teachers based on those standards, and foster high-quality professional development for teachers and school leaders.

The National Professional Standard for Principals, introduced in July 2011, is based on three requirements for leadership: vision and values; knowledge and comprehension; and personal qualities, and social and communication skills. These are made manifest in five areas of professional practice: leading teaching-learning processes; developing self and others; leading improvement, innovation and change; leading school management; and engaging and working with the community.

Excellence in school leadership

The standard for principals : The role in action

Leadership requirements

Professional practices:
- Vision and Values
- Knowledge and understanding
- Personal qualities, social and interpersonal skills
- High quality learning, teaching and schooling
- Successful learners, confident creative individuals and active informed citizens

- Leading teaching and learning
- Developing self and others
- Leading improvement, innovation and change
- Leading the management of the school
- Engaging and working with the community

Context: School, sector, community: socio-economic, geographic: and education systems at local, regional, national and global levels

Source: Adapted from Australian Institute for Teaching and School Leadership (2011).

Participation in professional development activities depends upon a variety of factors, including the availability of opportunities that are perceived to be relevant, the availability of time and other resources that would permit someone to take advantage of those opportunities, employers who are supportive, and the necessary qualifications to be able to benefit from the opportunities available. Figure 2.7 looks at the barriers to participating in professional development activities, according to principals' reports.

In 13 countries, more than half of school leaders agreed that their work schedule conflicted with opportunities for professional development. Among these countries, in Australia, Japan, Korea, Sweden and Alberta (Canada), more than 60% of school leaders agreed with this statement. On average across all participating countries and economies, 43% of principals reported that "conflicts with work schedule" prevent them from participating in professional development activities, while 13% reported that "conflicts with family responsibilities" prevent them from doing so.

Promoting effective school leadership   Chapter 2

Figure 2.7
Barriers to principals' participation in professional development

Percentage of lower secondary education principals who "strongly disagree", "disagree", "agree" or "strongly agree" that the following items present barriers to their participation in professional development

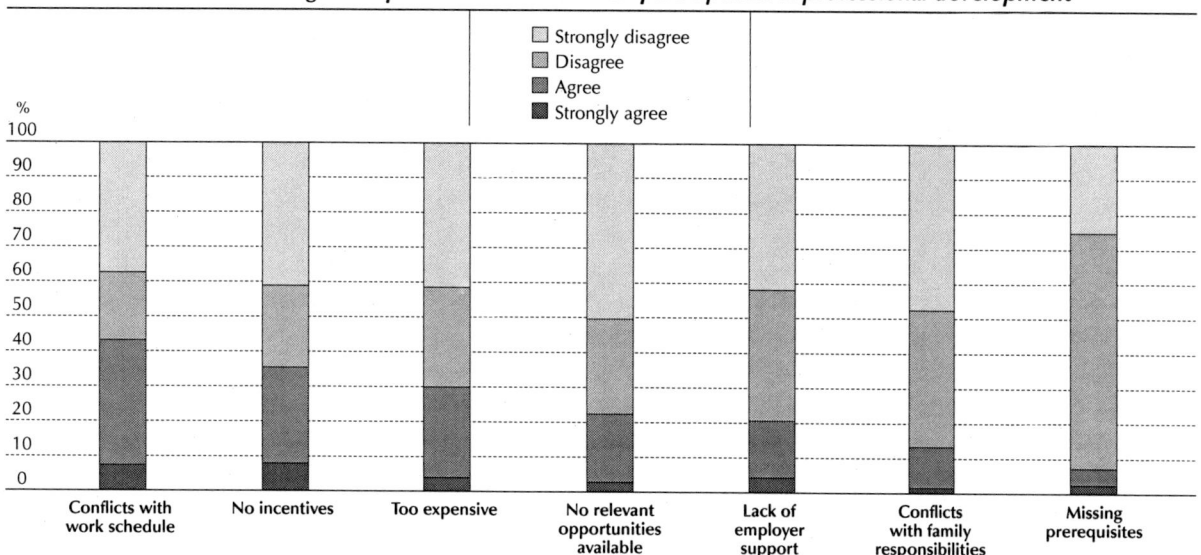

- Strongly disagree
- Disagree
- Agree
- Strongly agree

Categories (ranked): Conflicts with work schedule | No incentives | Too expensive | No relevant opportunities available | Lack of employer support | Conflicts with family responsibilities | Missing prerequisites

Items are ranked in descending order, based on the percentage of principals in lower secondary education who "strongly agree" or "agree" that the item presents a barrier to their participation in professional development.
Source: OECD, TALIS 2013 Database, Tables 3.15 and 3.15.Web.
StatLink http://dx.doi.org/10.1787/888933041402

Principals' engagement in professional development activities is an indicator of the value principals, and the people who employ principals, place on maintaining and developing professional knowledge. As mentioned earlier, because principals can have an impact on student achievement, improving the quality of school leadership is more important than improving the quality of a single teacher's practice (Branch et. al., 2013). It is thus important to stimulate interest in and opportunities for continuing professional development for principals and to remove the personal and professional barriers to participating in those activities.

PRINCIPALS' JOB SATISFACTION

Two aspects related to principals' job satisfaction were measured in TALIS: one is their satisfaction with their current work environment; the second is their satisfaction with the profession. Because the two were highly correlated, analyses were performed using the overall measure of principal job satisfaction, which combined these two aspects. Box 2.5 describes how TALIS measures job satisfaction.

Figure 2.8 looks at principals' reported levels of job satisfaction by country and, as indicated in Box 2.5, divides the responses in terms of principals' satisfaction with the profession as compared with their satisfaction with their current work environment (see also OECD, 2014, Table 3.26.Web). It is interesting to note that, across countries, there is more variation in principals' feelings about their profession than in their reported satisfaction with their schools. Across countries, around nine in ten principals are satisfied with their jobs overall and generally feel positive about their work environment at school. Moreover, when questioned about the profession of principal, in general, more than 80% of principals in all countries feel confident in their choice of career and do not regret having become a principal.

TALIS data were analysed to determine the relationship between instructional leadership and distributed leadership and principals' job satisfaction (OECD, 2014, Table 3.19). In 20 countries, principals who reported higher levels of instructional leadership tended to report that they are more satisfied with their job, while in 17 countries, principals who reported higher levels of distributed leadership tended to report that they are more satisfied with their jobs.

Additional factors affecting principals' job satisfaction were explored using multiple regression analyses with principals' job satisfaction as the dependent variable and demographic background (OECD, 2014, Table 3.20) and school background (OECD, 2014, Table 3.21) as independent variables.

> **Box 2.5. Description of the principal job satisfaction indices**
>
> Two aspects of principals' job satisfaction were measured in TALIS: satisfaction with the current work environment and satisfaction with the profession. Specifically, principals were asked to indicate how strongly they agreed or disagreed with the following statements as applied to their job. Response options ranged from strongly disagree to strongly agree.
>
> The first aspect (satisfaction with the current work environment) was measured with the following statements:
> - I enjoy working at this school.
> - I would recommend my school as a good place to work.
> - I am satisfied with my performance in this school.
> - All in all, I am satisfied with my job.
>
> The second aspect (satisfaction with the profession) was measured with the following statements:
> - The advantages of this profession clearly outweigh the disadvantages.
> - If I could decide again, I would still choose this job/position.
> - I regret that I decided to become a principal.
>
> Note that because these two aspects of job satisfaction are highly related to each other and perhaps overlap (see OECD, 2014, Table 3.37.Web), the overall job satisfaction scores are used in the analyses rather than the scores for each construct separately.
>
> **Source:** OECD (2014), *TALIS 2013 Results: An International Perspective on Teaching and Learning*, http://dx.doi.org/10.1787/9789264196261-en.

TALIS examines the relationship between job satisfaction and school characteristics, such as school locality, school type (public/private, source of funding), school size (number of staff and number of students) and student composition (percentage of students whose first language is different from the language of instruction, percentage of students with special needs, and percentage of students from socio-economically disadvantaged homes) (OECD, 2014, Table 3.21). While in most countries these variables were not related to job satisfaction, in a few countries some relationships emerged. For example, in Estonia, Alberta (Canada) and England (United Kingdom), principals working in schools with larger proportions of students with special needs tended to report less job satisfaction. The reverse is true in Australia and the Czech Republic. Furthermore, in Australia, principals working in schools with larger proportions of students from disadvantaged homes reported less job satisfaction. Policy makers in these countries might want to consider the support that they are providing to principals in these more challenging schools.

Analyses were also conducted to examine the relationship between job satisfaction and principals' reports of shortages of school resources (materials and personnel), delinquency in the school, the degree to which the school climate is characterised by mutual respect, and the proportion of administrative and support staff in the school (OECD, 2014, Table 3.22). The most pronounced relationship found was between having a school climate of mutual respect and principals' job satisfaction. Mutual respect is positively associated with principals' job satisfaction in all TALIS-participating countries and economies except Iceland, Latvia and Sweden. This means that principals tend to be satisfied with their job when there is a high level of mutual respect in school.

Given that between one in five and one in two principals reported resource shortages in the schools in which they work, it was surprising that, in many countries, those needs are not related to principals' job satisfaction.

The data allow for a further examination of the relationship between principals' job satisfaction and nine potential barriers to a principal's effectiveness (OECD, 2014, Table 3.23). These barriers include inadequate school budget and resources, government regulations and policy, teachers' absences, lack of parent involvement, teachers' career-based wage system, a lack of opportunities and support for principals' professional development, a lack of opportunities and support for teachers' professional development, a heavy workload and high level of responsibility, and a lack of shared leadership with other school staff members.

The one factor most commonly related to principals' job satisfaction is a heavy workload and high level of responsibility. In 14 countries, principals who identified heavier workloads as a barrier to their effectiveness also reported less job satisfaction. In nine countries, those principals who reported less distributed leadership among other school staff members also reported less job satisfaction.

Promoting effective school leadership

Chapter 2

Figure 2.8
Principals' job satisfaction
Percentage of lower secondary education principals who "agree" or "strongly agree" with the following statements

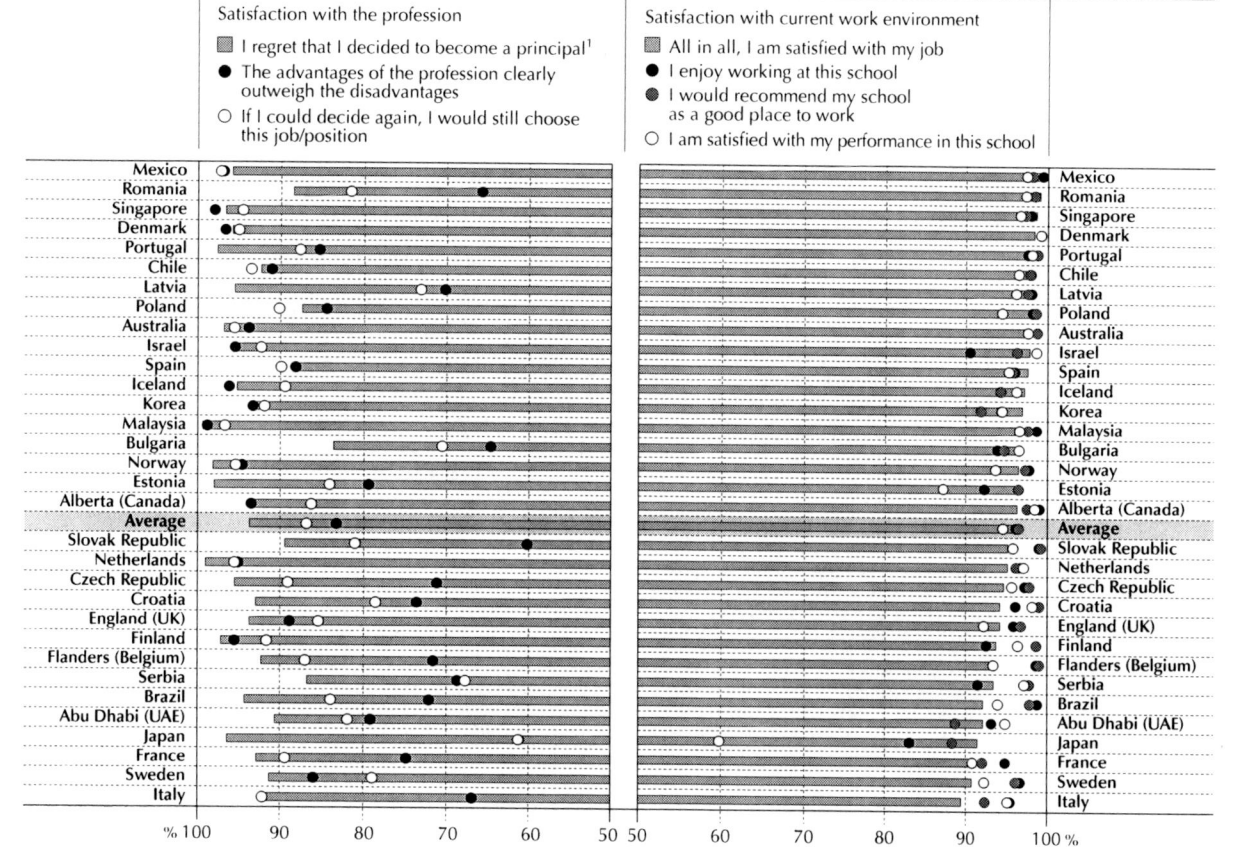

Satisfaction with the profession
- ▨ I regret that I decided to become a principal¹
- ● The advantages of the profession clearly outweigh the disadvantages
- ○ If I could decide again, I would still choose this job/position

Satisfaction with current work environment
- ▨ All in all, I am satisfied with my job
- ● I enjoy working at this school
- ● I would recommend my school as a good place to work
- ○ I am satisfied with my performance in this school

Countries (top to bottom): Mexico, Romania, Singapore, Denmark, Portugal, Chile, Latvia, Poland, Australia, Israel, Spain, Iceland, Korea, Malaysia, Bulgaria, Norway, Estonia, Alberta (Canada), Average, Slovak Republic, Netherlands, Czech Republic, Croatia, England (UK), Finland, Flanders (Belgium), Serbia, Brazil, Abu Dhabi (UAE), Japan, France, Sweden, Italy.

1. For the item "I regret that I decided to become a principal", the percentage represents the principals who answered "strongly disagree" or "disagree" because of the nature of the question.
Countries are ranked in descending order, based on the percentage of principals who "agree" or "strongly agree" that all in all, they are satisfied with their job.
Source: OECD, TALIS 2013 Database, Table 3.26.Web.
StatLink http://dx.doi.org/10.1787/888933041421

Few factors are consistently related to principals' job satisfaction across countries. One that is, however, is an atmosphere of mutual respect within the school. The most common factor affecting job satisfaction is, not surprisingly, a heavy workload. It is difficult to report with confidence which other factors are most strongly related to principals' job satisfaction when, for instance, larger proportions of students from disadvantaged homes or of students with special needs correlate with greater job satisfaction for some and less job satisfaction for others. Further investigation into the reasons behind these inconsistent attitudes might reveal significant differences in the support principals receive in more challenging circumstances.

WHO ARE TODAY'S SCHOOL LEADERS?

Who are the individuals who assume responsibility for such an extensive and significant range of tasks? What formal preparation and experience have they had? What do they do to grow or develop their professional practice? By learning more about the background, skills and experience of school leaders and examining the tasks that are required of them, countries can better understand where gaps in skills or experience might lie.

Age and gender of principals

The profile of school principals is relatively consistent across countries (Figure 2.9). Although principals are often former teachers – a profession in which, on average across TALIS-participating countries and economies, 68% of all teachers are female – the proportion of female principals is generally smaller than the proportion of male principals. Countries vary considerably, however, in how their principals are initially trained and how they later develop their professional skills.

SCHOOLS FOR 21ST-CENTURY LEARNERS: STRONG LEADERS, CONFIDENT TEACHERS, INNOVATIVE APPROACHES © OECD 2015

In some countries, many principals reported that they were offered little, no or weak preparation for assuming their role as school leaders. In addition, in many countries, because of a lack of opportunity, interest, time, prerequisites, incentives or encouragement, few principals participate in professional networks, mentoring or research activities. Principals also spend relatively little time in courses, conferences or observation visits. Given the importance of school leadership, countries may want to focus more on the preparation offered to prospective principals and on continuing professional development once individuals are appointed as principals.

Figure 2.9
Gender and age distribution of principals
Percentage of lower secondary education female principals and age of principals

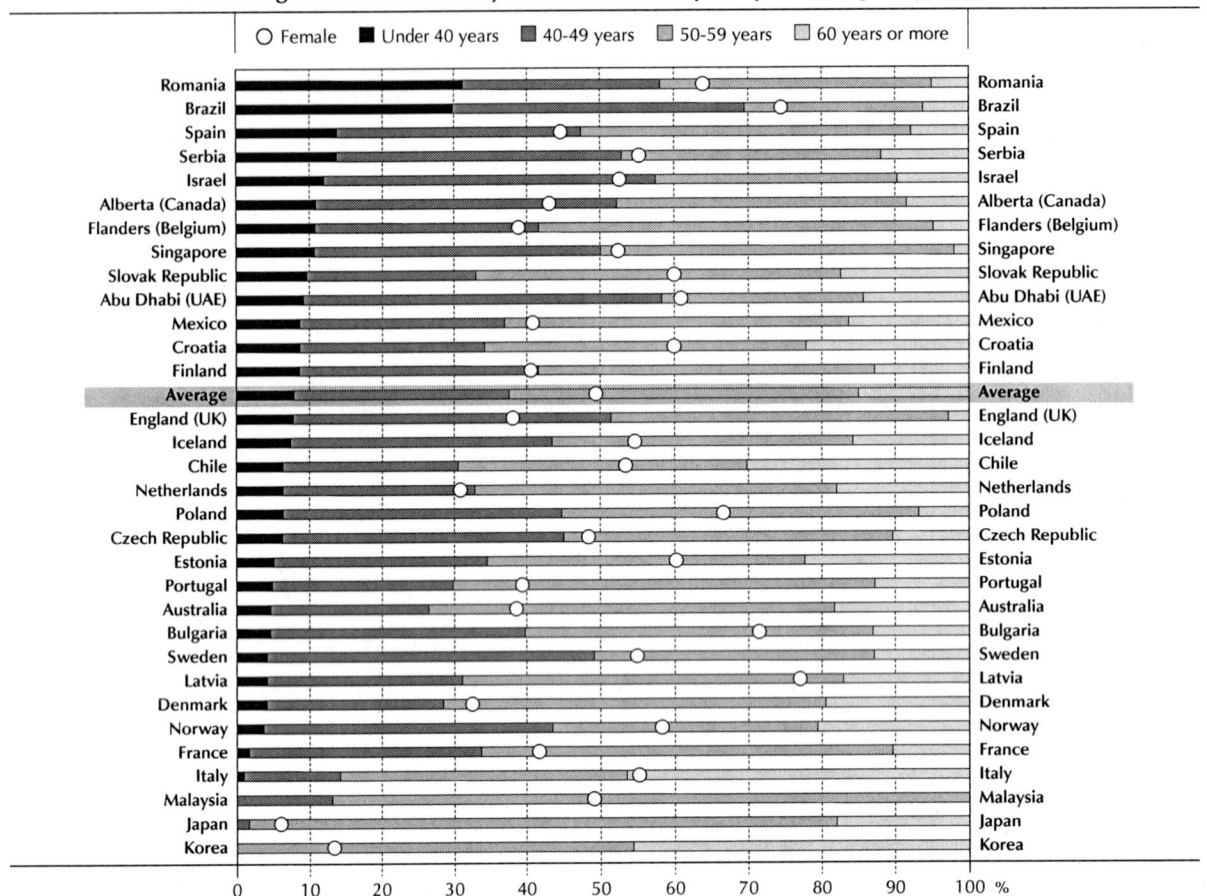

Countries are ranked in descending order, based on the percentage of principals who are under 40 years old.
Source: OECD, TALIS 2013 Database, Table 3.8.
StatLink http://dx.doi.org/10.1787/888933041307

Formal education of school principals

In the same way that the knowledge and skills students acquire from their schooling is influenced by the quality of the preparation and the conduct of teachers, the quality of a nation's schools depends on the preparation and conduct of its school leaders. Branch et al. (2013) argue that because school leaders have an impact on the achievement of all the students in a school, improving the quality of school leadership is more important than improving the quality of a *single* teacher's practice.

Given the complexity of their role and the fact that most principals typically begin their careers as teachers, it is not surprising that most principals (92% on average) are tertiary educated (ISCED level 5A, which typically includes Bachelor's degrees and Master's degrees from universities or equivalent institutions) (OECD, 2014, Table 3.9). In some countries, there are relatively large proportions of principals who have qualifications from a shorter, practically oriented tertiary programme (ISCED level 5B): Chile (25%), Croatia (18%), France (13%) and Flanders (Belgium) (40%).

Promoting effective school leadership

Chapter 2

TALIS 2013 also asked school leaders to report on their participation in school administration or principal-training programmes or courses, teacher-preparation programmes or courses and instructional-leadership training or courses (OECD, 2014, Table 3.10). Although one might assume that principal preparation would typically include these types of programmes or courses, one of the most striking findings, as shown in Figure 2.10, is the large proportion of school leaders in some countries who reported that their preparation did not include any of these.

Figure 2.10
Elements not included in principals' formal education
Percentage of lower secondary education principals who report that the following elements were not included in their formal education

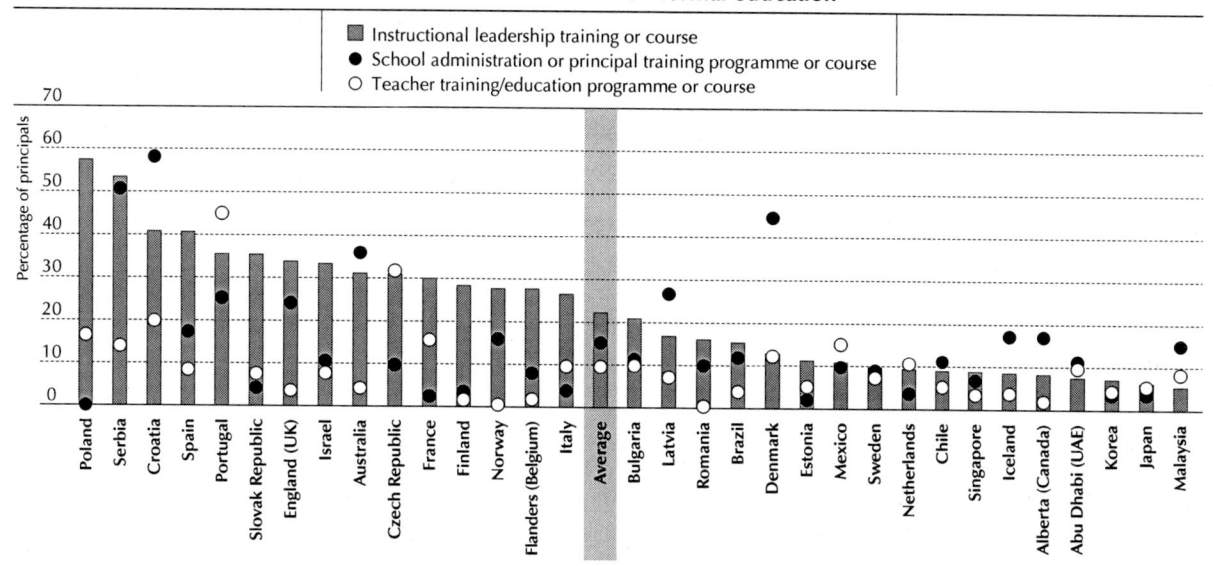

- Instructional leadership training or course
- School administration or principal training programme or course
- Teacher training/education programme or course

Countries are ranked in descending order, based on the percentage of principals for whom instructional leadership training or course were not included in their formal education.
Source: OECD, TALIS 2013 Database, Table 3.10.
StatLink http://dx.doi.org/10.1787/888933041326

On average across countries and economies that participated in TALIS, one in four principals reported that he or she had participated in a school administration programme or course before becoming principal, 37% reported that they had participated in such a programme after being appointed to the position, and 22% reported that they began such preparation prior to assuming their post and continued the preparation after being assigned as principal. However, in Croatia and Serbia, at least half of school principals reported that they had never participated in a school administration or principal-training programme or course.

Box 2.6. Sampling school leadership in Denmark

Denmark is introducing a "taster" course for aspiring school leaders. Danish teachers who may want to have a leadership position can begin to understand the different components of becoming a school leader through a "taster" course offered by local school districts or municipalities. Participants take part in one or more modules of a Leadership Diploma of Education. The course consists of theoretical assignments, case studies, personal reflections, discussions with a mentor about career opportunities, personal strengths and areas for development, and networking. Participants must also conduct a project in their own school. Those who want to continue can attend a two-year Diploma in Leadership course that includes seminars on economy, personal leadership, coaching, strategy implementation, change-management and problem-solving. The programme is managed by School Leadership Development, but is organised by the Local Government Training and Development Denmark, which is the centre for training and development for all of the country's municipalities and regions.

Source: Moos, L. (2011), "Educating Danish school leaders to meet new expectations?".

The data indicate that typical principal preparation includes participation in a teacher training or education programme (OECD, 2014, Table 3.10). Most principals participate in these programmes prior to assuming their responsibilities as principal. A substantial proportion of individuals participate in some formal preparation as teachers after they assume the principal's position (8%) or both before and after assuming that position (18%). However, 32% of the principals in the Czech Republic and 45% of the principals in Portugal reported that they had never participated in a teacher-training programme or course.

Similarly, principal preparation typically includes programmes in instructional leadership. On average, 24% of principals reported that they participated in such preparation prior to assuming the position, 31% reported participating after being appointed to the position, and 23% reported that they began such preparation prior to assuming their role as principal and continued the preparation after becoming principal. However, more than half of the principals in Poland and Serbia reported they had never participated in such preparation.

TALIS also measures the level or intensity of the leadership training in which principals had participated during in their formal education. Figure 2.11 shows the percentages of principals who reported that they received no, weak, average or strong leadership training as part of their formal education (OECD, 2014, Table 3.11). The level of leadership training is measured using the leadership training index, explained in Box 2.7.

Box 2.7. Construction of the leadership training index

The leadership training index presented in Table 3.11 was constructed from the question asking whether a principal's formal education included the following elements and whether this was before or after taking up duty as principal:

- school administration or principal training programme or course
- teacher training/education programme or course
- instructional leadership training or course

Responses indicating "never" were coded as zero (0), and responses indicating that the training had occurred "before", "after" or "before and after" were coded as one (1). Each respondent's codes were totalled to produce the following categories:

- 0 (no training)
- 1 (weak leadership training)
- 2 (average leadership training)
- 3 (strong leadership training)

Source: OECD (2014), *TALIS 2013 Results: An International Perspective on Teaching and Learning*, http://dx.doi.org/10.1787/9789264196261-en.

Box 2.8. Selecting and training school leaders in Singapore

To ensure that Singapore has the best school leaders, young teachers are continuously assessed for their leadership potential and are given the opportunity to develop their leadership capacity. Future school leaders are chosen from successful teachers already in the education system. Moreover, all education leadership positions are part of the teaching-career structure. Potential school leaders can serve on committees, be promoted to middle-level leadership positions (e.g. head of department), and be transferred to the ministry for a period.

Successful potential school leaders are selected to attend the Management and Leadership in Schools programme at Singapore's National Institute for Education, based on interviews and leadership-situation exercises. Once accepted, aspiring school leaders can attend the four-month executive leadership training. Potential vice-principals attend a six-month Leaders in Education programme. Candidates in both programmes are paid during their training. Only 35 people are selected for the executive leadership training each year.

More experienced school leaders mentor recently appointed leaders; and principals are periodically transferred among schools as part of Singapore's continuous improvement strategy. Experienced school leaders are offered the opportunity to become Cluster Superintendents, which is the first step towards a system-level leadership role.

Source: Mourshed, M., C. Chijioke and M. Barber (2010), "How the world's most improved school systems keep getting better", McKinsey and Company.

Promoting effective school leadership

More than 80% of principals in Chile, Estonia, Japan, Korea, the Netherlands and Singapore reported that they had strong leadership preparation as part of their formal education. The smallest proportions of principals who reported strong leadership preparation are found in Croatia (32%), Denmark (43%), Poland (41%), Portugal (40%) and Serbia (36%), including a number of principals who reported that they had received no formal administrative or principal-training preparation as part of their formal education.

Box 2.9. Leadership-preparation programmes in Finland and Norway

Finland started a programme in 2010 in 76 education networks to re-design the country's school leadership-development model. The main objective of the programme is to give greater responsibility to schools to implement staff-development activities that meet the individual or organisational needs of the school and its personnel. It also empowers teachers to create and implement their own professional-development programme. The programme initially targeted school leaders, teaching staff over 55 years of age, and persons who had not participated in professional-development activities in recent years. The programme encourages collaboration and the use of innovative learning methods and institutionalises professional development within the school.

In 2009, **Norway**'s central authorities introduced a new two-year programme to develop instructional leadership skills for school principals. The programme covers student learning outcomes and environment; management and administration; collaboration and organisation; guidance of teachers; development and change; and leadership identity. It was initially offered to new school principals with less than two years of experience, and will eventually be offered to more experienced school leaders as well.

Source: Hamalainen, K., K. Hamalainen and J. Kangasniemi (2011), "2011 Annual Conference of the Association for Teacher Education in Europe", 24-28 August 2011: 12 December 2011, "Osaava verme", 3 July 2011, http://ktl.jyu.fi/ktl/verme/osaavaverme; and OECD (2011).

Figure 2.11

Principals' formal education, including leadership training

Percentage of lower secondary education principals who report having received leadership training in their formal education[1]

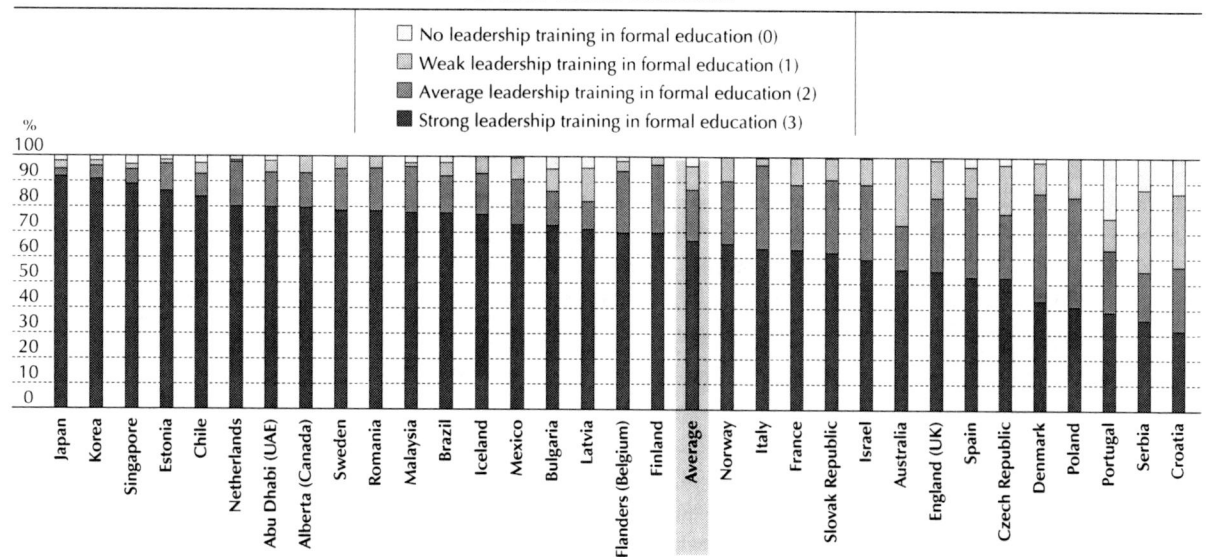

1. Leadership training index was constructed from the following variables: *i)* school administration or principal training programme or course; *ii)* teacher training/education programme or course; and *iii)* instructional leadership training or course. Responses indicating "never" were coded as zero (0) and responses indicating that the training had occurred "before", "after", or "before and after" were coded as one (1). Each respondent's codes were summed to produce the following categories: 0 (no training), 1 (weak leadership training), 2 (average leadership training) and 3 (strong leadership training). *Countries are ranked in descending order, based on the percentage of principals who received a strong leadership training in formal education.*
Source: OECD, TALIS 2013 Database, Table 3.11.
StatLink http://dx.doi.org/10.1787/888933041345

While there is merit in fostering different pathways to the goal of excellence in principal preparation, policy makers should look at exemplary programmes for guidance in developing such programmes. The Stanford Educational Leadership Institute study of exemplary programmes for the development of strong leaders has identified some characteristics common to exemplary programmes (Box 2.10).

Box 2.10. Characteristics of exemplary leadership programmes

Commissioned by the Wallace Foundation, a study by the Stanford Educational Leadership Institute examined eight exemplary pre-service and in-service programme models that develop strong educational leaders. All of the programmes of initial preparation that were characterised as exemplary shared the following characteristics:

- a comprehensive and coherent curriculum aligned with professional standards
- a philosophy and curriculum that explicitly focus on instructional leadership and school improvement
- student-centred instruction that integrates theory and practice and stimulates reflection
- faculty knowledgeable about their subject areas and experienced in school administration
- social and professional support in the form of a cohort structure and formalised mentoring and advising by expert principals
- vigorous, targeted recruitment and selection to seek out expert teachers with leadership potential
- well-designed and supervised administrative internships under the guidance of expert veterans.

Source: Darling-Hammond et al. (2007).

POLICY IMPLICATIONS

It is difficult to imagine that one person could have the expertise in all areas needed to successfully run a school, especially as some school systems continue to devolve and schools become more independent. School leaders must be visionary leaders who can inspire, motivate and develop their staff. They must be experts in the latest teaching, learning and assessment practices, and sensitive and adept human-resource managers who are able to provide feedback to staff that encourages them to grow. In addition, today's school principal must be able to bring together parents, community stakeholders, students, teachers and support staff into a community dedicated to the well-being of the school's students. In some cases, they may even be required to be a savvy businessperson, able to use the school's funds creatively for the most efficient and effective outcomes. Countries must consider how to train and develop people to be successful in such a challenging role; and school leaders themselves must try to find the right balance among their various responsibilities.

Empower teachers to play a role in decision making at the school level

Teacher leadership is important for many reasons. In all countries and economies that participated in TALIS, teachers who reported that they are given opportunities to participate in decision making at school also reported greater job satisfaction; in most countries, these teachers also reported greater confidence in their own ability to teach (self-efficacy). In addition, in almost all countries and economies, the extent to which teachers can participate in decision making was shown to have a strong, positive association with the likelihood that teachers reported that society values teaching as a profession.

Distributed leadership is not only important for helping to alleviate some of the burden imposed on school leaders, but it can be beneficial to teachers as well. Teachers are uniquely placed to participate in school-level decision making because they might be closer to students and parents, more familiar with how curriculum is implemented, and more knowledgeable about student assessments and results than their school principals might be. Policy makers should thus consider providing guidance on distributed leadership and distributed decision making at the system level.

Encourage the practice of distributed leadership

Given a principal's importance to the school's operations and a principal's impact on instruction, it is important that being a principal is, and remains, satisfying work. Principals who feel that there is a climate of mutual respect in their schools reported greater job satisfaction. Through their work and the relationships they establish with teachers, staff and students, principals can help to create a positive, mutually supportive climate that, in turn, contributes to their satisfaction.

This is likely why successful professional practice is also dependent on personal qualities and social and interpersonal skills. But these personal qualities and social and interpersonal skills must be complemented by vision and values, as well as by knowledge and understanding, and be put to the service of learning and teaching, the professional development of oneself and others, improving and innovating, managing the school, and engaging and working with the community.

Develop formal programmes to prepare school leaders to enter the profession

The responsibilities of principals are many and complex; yet there is wide variation within countries in the degree to which school principals participate in school-administration or principal-training programmes or courses, teacher-preparation programmes or courses, and instructional-leadership training or courses. Many principals reported that their preparation did not include these experiences. Over time, countries are likely to reap enormous benefits, in terms of school improvement and student achievement, from developing quality professional-preparation programmes for their school principals.

Provide opportunities for, and remove barriers to, continuing professional development for principals

Keeping one's professional knowledge and practice up-to-date is affected by many different factors, including the opportunities that are available, and having the time and qualifications necessary to take advantage of the opportunities provided. The proportions of principals who reported that they had engaged in collaborative professional development activities during the 12 months prior to the survey, and the average number of days spent by those who participated, vary considerably. In many countries, large proportions of principals reported that there were no relevant opportunities available for professional development and no incentives to participate. In more than a dozen countries, principals said their work schedules conflicted with opportunities for professional development. Countries should strive to minimise obstacles to professional development for principals, align state-supported opportunities with the country's long-term education goals (OECD, 2013), and set standards for high-quality professional learning. Since what principals do affects the achievement of all the students in a school, principals must make improving their practice a priority and must take advantage of the opportunities available.

There are several high-priority areas for professional development. For example, instructional leadership can improve student achievement by:

- establishing the school outcomes that are essential for all students
- ensuring that these outcomes are expressed clearly in the curriculum and are supported with appropriate instructional material
- holding students, parents and teachers accountable for those outcomes
- encouraging and coaching teachers' use of teaching strategies that improve learning outcomes for all students
- assessing student progress in the areas of importance at different times over their school careers (Ungerleider, 2006; Ungerleider, 2003; Willms, 2000; Willms, 1998; Woessman 2001).

Ensure that principals receive training in, and have opportunities to assume, instructional leadership

It could be said that instructional leadership – focusing on the teaching and learning that take place in school – is the most important of all principals' tasks. TALIS data show that when principals reported higher levels of instructional leadership, they were also more likely to develop a professional-development plan for their school (13 countries), observe teaching in the classroom as part of a teacher's formal appraisal (20 countries), and report that there is high level of mutual respect among colleagues at the school (17 countries). Principals who reported higher levels of instructional leadership also tended to spend more time on curriculum and teaching-related tasks and reported greater job satisfaction.

Yet, more than one in five (22%) principals reported that they had never participated in instructional training, and 31% reported that they had participated in such training only after they became a principal.

Countries need to review instructional leadership training for principals and how principals actually assume that leadership role at school. While more instructional leadership training is needed, principals also need to be made aware of its importance and be offered this training during their initial principal training as well.

Notes

1. In the analyses, the categories "often" and "very often" were collapsed into one category, called "frequently". The categories "never or rarely" and "sometimes" were combined into one category, called "infrequently".

> **Note regarding Israel**
> The statistical data for Israel are supplied by and under the responsibility of the relevant Israeli authorities. The use of such data by the OECD is without prejudice to the status of the Golan Heights, East Jerusalem and Israeli settlements in the West Bank under the terms of international law.

References

Biniaminov, I. and N.S. Glasman (1983), "School determinants of student achievement in secondary education", *American Educational Research Journal*, Vol. 20/2, pp. 251-268.

Branch, G.F., E.A. Hanushek and S.G. Rivkin (2013), "School leaders matter: Measuring the impact of effective principals", *Education Next*, Vol. 13/1, pp. 63-69.

Darling-Hammond, L. et al. (2007), *Preparing School Leaders for a Changing World: Lessons from Exemplary Leadership Development Programs*, Stanford Educational Leadership Institute, Stanford University, Stanford, CA.

DuFour, R. (2004), "What is a professional learning community?", *Educational Leadership*, Vol. 61/8, pp. 6-11.

Epstein, R.M. and E.M. Hundert (2002), "Defining and assessing professional competence", *Journal of the American Medical Association*, Vol. 287/2, pp. 226-235.

Gerrard, S. (2012), "A response to raven", *The Psychology of Education Review*, Vol. 36/1, pp. 27-30.

Goode, W.J. (1969), "The theoretical limits of professionalism", in A. Etzioni (ed.), *The Semi-Professions and Their Organizations: Teachers, Nurses, and Social Workers*, Free Press, New York, NY.

Grissom, J.A., S. Loeb and B. Master (2013), "Effective instructional time use for school leaders: Longitudinal evidence from observations of principals", *Educational Researcher*, Vol. 42/8, pp. 433-444.

Harris, A. (2012), "Distributed leadership: Implications for the role of the principal", *Journal of Management Development*, Vol. 31/1, pp. 7-17.

Harris, A. (2008), *Distributed Leadership: Developing Tomorrow's Leaders*, Routledge, London.

Huang, F.L. and T.R. Moon (2009), "Is experience the best teacher? A multilevel analysis of teacher characteristics and student achievement in low performing schools", *Educational Assessment, Evaluation and Accountability*, Vol. 21, pp. 209-234.

Jepsen, C. and S. Rivkin (2009), "Class size reduction and student achievement: The potential tradeoff between teacher quality and class size", *Journal of Human Resources*, Vol. 44/1, pp. 223-250.

Jeynes, W.H. (2011), *Parental Involvement and Academic Success*, Routledge, New York, NY.

Larson, M.S. (1977), *The Rise of Professionalism: A Sociological Analysis*, University of California Press, Berkeley, CA.

Leithwood, K., B. Mascall and T. Strauss (2009), *Distributed Leadership According to the Evidence*, Routledge, London.

Lieberman, A. and L. Miller (2004), *Teacher Leadership*, Jossey-Bass, San Francisco, CA.

MacNeil, A.J. and D. Prater (1999), "Teachers and principals differ on the seriousness of school discipline: A national perspective", *National Forum of Applied Educational Research Journal*, Vol. 12/3, pp. 1-7.

Moos, L. (2011), "Educating Danish school leaders to meet new expectations?", *School Leadership & Management*, Vol. 31, Issue 2.

Mourshed, M., C. Chijioke and M. Barber (2010), "How the world's most improved school systems keep getting better", McKinsey and Company.

OECD (2014), *TALIS 2013 Results: An International Perspective on Teaching and Learning*, OECD Publishing, Paris, http://dx.doi.org/10.1787/9789264196261-en.

OECD (2013), *OECD Reviews of Evaluation and Assessment in Education. Synergies for Better Learning: An International Perspective on Evaluation and Assessment*, OECD Publishing, Paris, http://dx.doi.org/10.1787/9789264190658-en.

Pont, B., D. Nusche and H. Moorman (2008), *Improving School Leadership, Volume 1: Policy and Practice*, OECD Publishing, Paris, http://dx.doi.org/10.1787/9789264044715-en.

Schleicher, A. (ed.) (2012), *Preparing Teachers and Developing School Leaders for the 21st Century: Lessons from around the World*, OECD Publishing, Paris, http://dx.doi.org/10.1787/9789264174559-en.

Smylie, M.A. et al. (2007), "Trust and the development of distributed leadership", *Journal of School Leadership*, Vol. 17/4, pp. 469-503.

Ungerleider, C.S. (2006), "Reflections on the use of large-scale student assessment for improving student success", *Canadian Journal of Education*, Vol. 29/3, pp. 873-888.

Ungerleider, C.S. (2003), "Large-scale student assessment: Guidelines for policy-makers", *International Journal of Testing*, Vol. 3/2, pp. 119-128.

Vanhoof, J. et al. (2014), "Data use by Flemish school principals: Impact of attitude, self-efficacy and external expectations", *Educational Studies*, Vol. 40/1, pp. 48-62.

Veenman, S., Y. Visser and N. Wijkamp (1998), "Implementation effects of a program for the training of coaching skills with school principals", *School Effectiveness and School Improvement: An International Journal of Research, Policy and Practice*, Vol. 9/2, pp. 135-156.

Veldman, D.J. and J.E. Brophy (1974), "Measuring teacher effects on pupil achievement", *Journal of Educational Psychology*, Vol. 66/3, pp. 319-324.

Willms, J.D. (2000), "Monitoring school performance for 'standards-based reform'", *Evaluation and Research in Education*, Vol. 14/3 and 14/4, pp. 237-253.

Willms, J.D. (1998), "Assessment strategies for Title I of the improving America's Schools Act", report prepared for the Committee on Title I Testing and Assessment of the National Academy of Sciences.

Woessmann, L. (2001), *Schooling, Resources, Educational Institutions, and Student Performance: The International Evidence*, Kiel Institute of World Economics, Kiel.

Further reading

Bangs, J. and D. Frost (2012), "Teacher self-efficacy, voice and leadership: Towards a policy framework for Education International", University of Cambridge, Cambridge.

Burns, D. and L. Darling-Hammond (2014), *Teaching Around the World: What Can TALIS Tell Us?*, Stanford Center for Opportunity Policy in Education, Stanford, CA.

Frost, D. (2011), *Supporting Teacher Leadership in 15 Countries: The International Teacher Leadership project, Phase 1 – A report*, Leadership for Learning University of Cambridge Faculty of Education, Cambridge, United Kingdom.

Lieberman, A. and L. Miller (2004), *Teacher Leadership*, Jossey-Bass, San Francisco, CA.

Chapter 3

STRENGTHENING TEACHERS' CONFIDENCE IN THEIR OWN ABILITIES

This chapter focuses on teachers' self-efficacy: teachers' confidence in their own abilities to teach. Based on data from the 2013 Teaching and Learning International Survey (TALIS), the chapter examines some of the factors that can affect teachers' self-efficacy, including the classroom environment, relations with colleagues and students, appraisal and feedback, collaboration with other teachers, and teachers' own beliefs and practices.

Chapter 3: Strengthening teachers' confidence in their own abilities

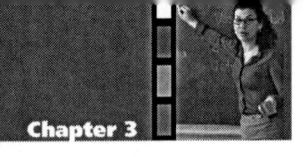

Evidence from PISA and TALIS suggests that the most successful education systems are those in countries/economies whose society values the teaching profession (Figure 3.1).

However, the TALIS 2013 survey finds that fewer than one in three teachers believes that teaching is a valued profession in society (Figure 3.2). In all but one of the countries and economies that participated in TALIS, the extent to which teachers can participate in decision making has a strong, positive association with the likelihood of reporting that teaching is valued by society.

Figure 3.1
Relationship between the value of the teaching profession and the share of top mathematics performers

Relationship between lower secondary education teachers' view on the value of their profession in society and the share of top mathematics performers in PISA 2012

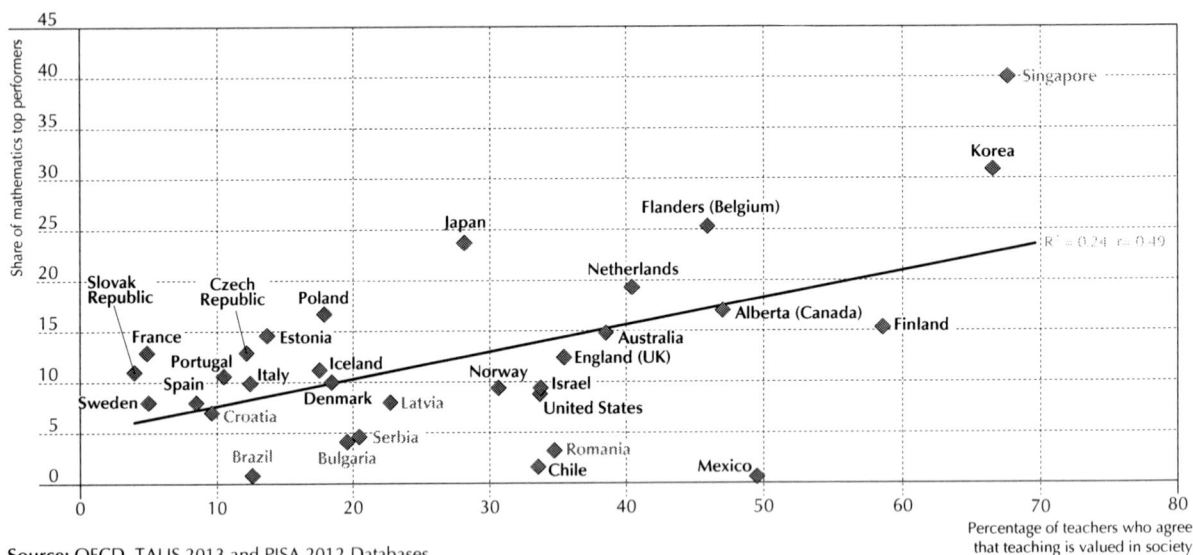

Source: OECD, TALIS 2013 and PISA 2012 Databases.
StatLink http://dx.doi.org/10.1787/888933199422

In examining teachers' self-efficacy (teachers' self-confidence in their own ability to teach) and the factors that shape teachers' sense of self-efficacy, TALIS finds that:

- In all countries/economies surveyed, teachers who reported that they are given opportunities to participate in decision making at school also reported greater job satisfaction and, in most countries, greater self-efficacy. The relationship between job satisfaction and teacher participation in school decision making is particularly strong in all countries.

- With more teaching experience comes a greater sense of self-efficacy but, in some cases, less job satisfaction. In 26 countries, teachers with more than five years of work experience reported greater self-efficacy than their less-experienced colleagues; but in 12 countries, these teachers reported less job satisfaction.

- Challenging classroom circumstances can affect teachers' sense of self-efficacy and job satisfaction. In particular, in almost all countries, an increase in the percentage of students with behavioural problems is associated with a strong decrease in teachers' reported levels of job satisfaction.

- In nearly all countries, teachers' perception that appraisal and feedback lead to changes in their teaching practice is related to greater job satisfaction; but in every country and economy that participated in TALIS, teachers' perception that appraisal and feedback is performed merely for administrative purposes is related to less job satisfaction.

- Positive interpersonal relationships with the school leader, other teachers, and students can mitigate the otherwise detrimental effects that challenging classrooms might have on a teacher's satisfaction with his or her job or feelings of self-efficacy. Relationships between teachers and students are particularly strongly related to teachers' job satisfaction.

- Collaboration among teachers, whether through professional learning or collaborative practices, is also related to higher levels of both self-efficacy and job satisfaction. In particular, teachers who reported that they participate in collaborative professional learning activities five times a year or more also reported significantly higher levels of self-efficacy (in almost all countries) and greater job satisfaction (in two out of three of the participating countries/economies).

Strengthening teachers' confidence in their own abilities Chapter 3

Figure 3.2
Teachers' view of how society values the teaching profession

Percentage of lower secondary education teachers who "strongly disagree", "disagree", "agree" or "strongly agree" with the following statement: I think that the teaching profession is valued in society

Legend: Strongly disagree / Disagree / Agree / Strongly agree

Countries (in order shown): Malaysia, Singapore, Korea, Abu Dhabi (UAE), Finland, Mexico, Alberta (Canada), Flanders (Belgium), Netherlands, Australia, England (UK), Romania, Israel, Chile, **Average**, Norway, Japan, Latvia, Serbia, Bulgaria, Denmark, Poland, Iceland, Estonia, Brazil, Italy, Czech Republic, Portugal, Croatia, Spain, Sweden, France, Slovak Republic.

Percentage of teachers (0–100)

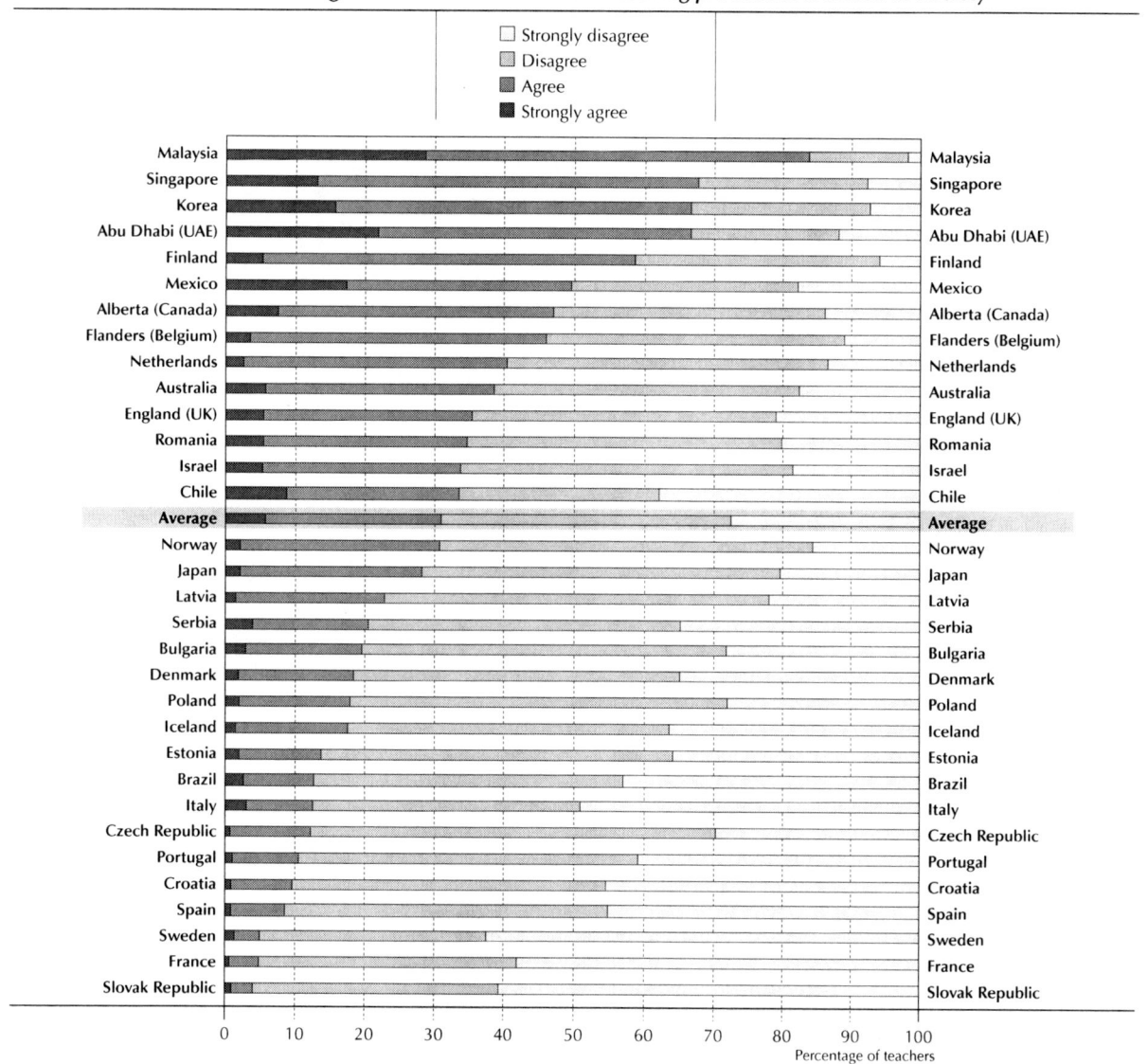

Countries are ranked in descending order, based on the percentage of teachers who "strongly agree" or "agree" that they think that the teaching profession is valued in society.
Source: OECD, TALIS 2013 Database, Tables 7.2 and 7.2.Web.
StatLink http://dx.doi.org/10.1787/888933042219

WHY SELF-EFFICACY MATTERS

PISA data show how students' self-efficacy – their belief in their own ability – has a significant influence on their academic achievement and behaviour. Similarly, there is evidence that teachers' sense of self-efficacy – their belief in their ability to teach, engage students and manage a classroom – has an impact on student achievement and motivation, as well as on teachers' own practices, enthusiasm, commitment, job satisfaction and behaviour in the classroom (Skaalvik and Skaalvik, 2007; Tschannen-Moran and Woolfolk Hoy, 2001; Tschannen-Moran and Barr, 2004; Caprara et al., 2006). A poor sense of self-efficacy, for example, has been linked to teachers having more difficulties with student misbehaviour, being more pessimistic about student learning, and experiencing higher levels of job-related stress and less job satisfaction (Caprara et al., 2003; Caprara et al., 2006; Klassen and Chiu, 2010; Collie et al., 2012). TALIS asked teachers a range of questions about specific aspects of their sense of self-efficacy (see Box 3.1).

Box 3.1. Teachers' self-efficacy and job satisfaction indices

TALIS measures three aspects of teacher self-efficacy: classroom management, instruction and student engagement. Similarly, TALIS measures two aspects of teachers' job satisfaction: satisfaction with the profession and satisfaction with the current work environment.

Efficacy in classroom management
- Control disruptive behaviour in the classroom.
- Make my expectations about student behaviour clear.
- Get students to follow classroom rules.
- Calm a student who is disruptive or noisy.

Efficacy in instruction
- Craft good questions for my students.
- Use a variety of assessment strategies.
- Provide an alternative explanation, for example, when students are confused.
- Implement alternative instructional strategies in my classroom.

Efficacy in student engagement
- Get students to believe they can do well in school work.
- Help my students value learning.
- Motivate students who show low interest in school work.
- Help students think critically.

Satisfaction with current work environment
- I would like to change to another school if that were possible.
- I enjoy working at this school.
- I would recommend my school as a good place to work.
- All in all, I am satisfied with my job.

Satisfaction with profession
- The advantages of being a teacher clearly outweigh the disadvantages.
- If I could decide again, I would still choose to work as a teacher.
- I regret that I decided to become a teacher.
- I wonder whether it would have been better to choose another profession.

Source: OECD (2014), *TALIS 2013 Results: An International Perspective on Teaching and Learning*, http://dx.doi.org/10.1787/9789264196261-en.

The individual items that make up the indices discussed in Box 3.1 are interesting in and of themselves. Figure 3.3 shows that in the majority of the countries and economies that participated in TALIS, most teachers reported holding beliefs that suggest high levels of self-efficacy. On average across countries, between 80% and 92% of teachers reported that they can often get students to believe they can do well in school, help students value learning, craft good questions for students, control disruptive behaviour in the classroom, make clear their expectations for student behaviour, help students think critically, get students to follow classroom rules, calm a student who is disruptive, use a variety of assessment strategies, and provide alternative explanations when students are confused.[1] In comparison, motivating students who show low interest in school work (70%) and implementing alternative instructional strategies (77%) both seem relatively more difficult for teachers across TALIS-participating countries/economies to achieve.

Yet in some countries, teachers seem to believe significantly and consistently less in their abilities in these domains, compared with the average. Notably, teachers in Japan reported lower levels of confidence in their ability across domains as compared with the TALIS average. The averages range from a low of only 16% of teachers in Japan believing they can often help students to think critically, to a high of 54% who think that they can provide alternative explanations when students are confused. Teachers in the Czech Republic also reported less confidence in their abilities in some areas.

Strengthening teachers' confidence in their own abilities — Chapter 3

For example, only 30% of teachers in the Czech Republic believe that they can motivate students who show low interest in school work, while 39% think that they can help students value learning. The patterns are less consistent among teachers in Croatia, Norway and Spain; but in each of these countries, 53% of teachers or less responded positively to one or more of the statements used to measure self-efficacy.

Figure 3.3 (1/2)
Teachers' self-efficacy
Percentage of lower secondary education teachers who feel they can do the following "quite a bit" or "a lot"

	Get students to believe they can do well in school work %	S.E.	Help my students value learning %	S.E.	Craft good questions for my students %	S.E.	Control disruptive behaviour in the classroom %	S.E.	Motivate students who show low interest in school work %	S.E.	Make my expectations about student behaviour clear %	S.E.
Australia	86.9	(1.1)	81.3	(1.4)	86.0	(0.8)	86.7	(0.7)	65.8	(1.3)	93.4	(0.8)
Brazil	96.5	(0.2)	94.8	(0.3)	97.5	(0.2)	89.7	(0.5)	87.6	(0.6)	96.8	(0.3)
Bulgaria	91.7	(0.7)	94.9	(0.5)	82.3	(0.9)	86.4	(0.8)	67.8	(1.2)	97.1	(0.4)
Chile	90.6	(0.9)	91.0	(1.0)	91.3	(0.9)	90.7	(1.1)	82.9	(1.1)	93.3	(0.8)
Croatia	68.6	(1.0)	52.1	(0.9)	90.3	(0.5)	83.0	(0.7)	50.7	(1.0)	93.6	(0.4)
Cyprus*	95.8	(0.5)	94.2	(0.6)	95.1	(0.5)	93.3	(0.7)	85.3	(0.9)	96.2	(0.5)
Czech Republic	50.5	(0.9)	39.0	(1.0)	70.9	(1.0)	77.1	(0.9)	30.0	(1.0)	71.9	(0.9)
Denmark	99.0	(0.2)	96.6	(0.6)	96.3	(0.5)	96.3	(0.6)	82.5	(0.9)	98.8	(0.3)
Estonia	81.3	(0.8)	86.0	(0.6)	74.4	(0.9)	76.7	(1.0)	75.0	(0.9)	86.9	(0.7)
Finland	83.9	(0.8)	77.3	(0.8)	90.1	(0.5)	86.3	(0.8)	60.4	(1.1)	92.7	(0.5)
France	95.2	(0.5)	87.1	(0.7)	93.8	(0.5)	94.6	(0.5)	76.6	(0.9)	97.7	(0.3)
Iceland	88.6	(1.0)	82.5	(1.1)	96.1	(0.5)	89.9	(0.9)	72.1	(1.3)	91.2	(0.9)
Israel	92.1	(0.5)	85.4	(0.9)	89.8	(0.8)	85.0	(0.9)	74.9	(1.1)	94.1	(0.5)
Italy	98.0	(0.3)	95.6	(0.3)	93.8	(0.5)	93.5	(0.5)	87.3	(0.7)	93.4	(0.5)
Japan	17.6	(0.7)	26.0	(0.9)	42.8	(1.0)	52.7	(1.0)	21.9	(0.8)	53.0	(1.0)
Korea	78.7	(1.0)	78.3	(0.9)	77.4	(0.9)	76.3	(1.1)	59.9	(1.0)	70.5	(1.1)
Latvia	91.0	(0.8)	78.6	(1.2)	93.5	(0.6)	85.2	(1.0)	64.8	(1.5)	94.3	(0.6)
Malaysia	95.9	(0.4)	98.0	(0.3)	95.8	(0.4)	96.3	(0.4)	95.2	(0.4)	92.2	(0.5)
Mexico	87.8	(0.6)	91.0	(0.6)	85.2	(0.8)	86.0	(0.7)	79.1	(0.9)	87.4	(0.8)
Netherlands	90.0	(0.9)	70.2	(1.6)	88.2	(1.1)	89.2	(0.9)	62.5	(1.5)	95.3	(0.6)
Norway	79.9	(1.0)	60.9	(1.9)	79.0	(1.4)	83.8	(0.7)	38.8	(1.0)	89.7	(0.7)
Poland	80.7	(0.8)	67.7	(1.0)	79.4	(0.8)	88.3	(0.9)	59.8	(1.1)	94.6	(0.6)
Portugal	98.9	(0.2)	99.0	(0.2)	98.2	(0.3)	96.1	(0.3)	93.8	(0.5)	96.9	(0.4)
Romania	97.9	(0.4)	95.1	(0.5)	98.9	(0.2)	97.8	(0.3)	88.7	(0.7)	98.5	(0.2)
Serbia	84.9	(0.6)	76.1	(0.7)	90.0	(0.7)	86.1	(0.6)	63.4	(0.9)	91.9	(0.5)
Singapore	83.9	(0.7)	81.5	(0.8)	81.2	(0.7)	79.5	(0.7)	72.1	(0.9)	89.0	(0.6)
Slovak Republic	92.5	(0.5)	88.5	(0.7)	94.5	(0.4)	91.1	(0.7)	84.9	(0.8)	96.9	(0.4)
Spain	71.1	(1.0)	74.1	(0.9)	86.3	(0.7)	81.5	(0.8)	53.4	(1.1)	90.1	(0.7)
Sweden	93.9	(0.5)	76.6	(1.0)	82.0	(0.8)	84.9	(0.8)	64.1	(1.0)	90.6	(0.6)
Sub-national entities												
Abu Dhabi (United Arab Emirates)	96.3	(0.5)	95.4	(0.6)	94.8	(0.5)	94.4	(0.7)	94.9	(0.5)	96.7	(0.4)
Alberta (Canada)	87.0	(0.9)	79.2	(1.1)	84.1	(1.0)	86.9	(0.9)	60.6	(1.3)	95.4	(0.5)
England (United Kingdom)	93.0	(0.6)	87.0	(0.8)	89.8	(0.9)	88.7	(0.8)	75.7	(0.9)	95.6	(0.5)
Flanders (Belgium)	93.1	(0.5)	81.6	(0.8)	95.1	(0.4)	96.4	(0.4)	77.7	(0.9)	97.2	(0.3)
Average	85.8	(0.1)	80.7	(0.2)	87.4	(0.1)	87.0	(0.1)	70.0	(0.2)	91.3	(0.1)
United States	83.7	(1.1)	74.9	(1.3)	88.0	(1.2)	86.2	(1.1)	61.9	(1.4)	94.9	(0.6)

*See notes at the end of this chapter.
Source: OECD, TALIS 2013 Database.
StatLink http://dx.doi.org/10.1787/888933047463

Chapter 3
Strengthening teachers' confidence in their own abilities

Figure 3.3 (2/2)
Teachers' self-efficacy
Percentage of lower secondary education teachers who feel they can do the following "quite a bit" or "a lot"

	Help students think critically %	S.E.	Get students to follow classroom rules %	S.E.	Calm a student who is disruptive or noisy %	S.E.	Use a variety of assessment strategies %	S.E.	Provide an alternative explanation for an example when students are confused %	S.E.	Implement alternative instructional strategies in my classroom %	S.E.
Australia	78.4	(1.3)	89.4	(0.9)	83.6	(1.1)	86.3	(1.1)	94.0	(0.7)	82.7	(1.0)
Brazil	95.1	(0.3)	91.7	(0.4)	90.2	(0.5)	91.3	(0.5)	97.7	(0.2)	87.9	(0.6)
Bulgaria	82.5	(0.9)	96.1	(0.4)	87.9	(0.8)	87.8	(0.8)	95.9	(0.4)	69.6	(1.1)
Chile	90.2	(0.9)	92.8	(1.0)	89.2	(1.0)	89.3	(0.9)	95.3	(0.6)	88.9	(1.0)
Croatia	77.9	(0.7)	83.1	(0.6)	81.2	(0.7)	84.6	(0.6)	96.4	(0.4)	92.3	(0.5)
Cyprus*	94.6	(0.6)	96.2	(0.6)	90.2	(0.7)	87.3	(0.9)	97.2	(0.4)	88.1	(0.9)
Czech Republic	51.8	(1.2)	76.4	(1.0)	77.1	(1.0)	72.0	(1.1)	85.2	(0.8)	52.2	(1.1)
Denmark	92.8	(0.7)	94.9	(0.7)	94.3	(0.6)	79.5	(1.1)	98.0	(0.4)	86.6	(1.1)
Estonia	74.8	(0.9)	83.5	(0.8)	73.9	(0.9)	72.3	(0.9)	78.6	(0.9)	59.8	(1.1)
Finland	72.8	(1.0)	86.6	(0.8)	77.1	(0.9)	64.2	(1.1)	76.9	(0.9)	68.2	(1.1)
France	88.7	(0.7)	98.2	(0.3)	94.9	(0.5)	88.3	(0.7)	98.5	(0.2)	82.2	(0.8)
Iceland	74.6	(1.2)	92.1	(0.8)	88.2	(1.0)	85.7	(1.0)	91.8	(0.8)	77.4	(1.2)
Israel	77.6	(1.1)	86.6	(0.8)	81.0	(0.8)	75.0	(1.3)	92.5	(0.5)	77.8	(1.0)
Italy	94.9	(0.4)	96.7	(0.3)	89.7	(0.6)	90.9	(0.6)	98.3	(0.2)	91.3	(0.5)
Japan	15.6	(0.6)	48.8	(1.1)	49.9	(1.1)	26.7	(0.8)	54.2	(0.8)	43.6	(0.9)
Korea	63.6	(1.1)	80.5	(1.0)	73.1	(1.1)	66.6	(1.2)	81.4	(0.9)	62.5	(1.1)
Latvia	83.0	(1.1)	92.0	(0.8)	81.2	(0.9)	90.1	(0.7)	91.4	(0.7)	62.1	(1.4)
Malaysia	91.9	(0.5)	98.0	(0.3)	96.8	(0.3)	88.6	(0.6)	95.8	(0.4)	89.5	(0.5)
Mexico	88.8	(0.7)	85.0	(0.7)	78.0	(1.0)	83.9	(0.8)	93.7	(0.4)	87.5	(0.8)
Netherlands	77.8	(1.2)	90.6	(0.9)	86.7	(0.9)	66.7	(1.6)	93.0	(0.8)	62.2	(1.3)
Norway	66.6	(1.8)	85.6	(0.9)	84.3	(0.8)	73.4	(1.6)	87.8	(1.1)	66.0	(1.5)
Poland	77.5	(0.8)	91.3	(0.7)	87.2	(0.8)	86.7	(0.6)	87.4	(0.6)	66.0	(1.0)
Portugal	97.5	(0.3)	97.5	(0.2)	95.2	(0.4)	98.3	(0.3)	99.2	(0.2)	95.9	(0.3)
Romania	93.4	(0.6)	97.7	(0.4)	97.7	(0.3)	98.0	(0.3)	99.4	(0.2)	93.2	(0.6)
Serbia	84.3	(0.7)	91.1	(0.5)	85.6	(0.6)	86.3	(0.7)	95.3	(0.4)	74.1	(0.8)
Singapore	74.9	(0.7)	83.5	(0.6)	75.3	(0.7)	71.6	(0.9)	88.5	(0.6)	72.8	(0.8)
Slovak Republic	90.2	(0.8)	95.3	(0.4)	92.2	(0.6)	92.0	(0.6)	95.1	(0.4)	80.6	(0.8)
Spain	78.9	(0.9)	83.8	(0.8)	73.7	(0.9)	87.0	(0.6)	96.5	(0.4)	83.2	(0.8)
Sweden	75.1	(0.9)	86.5	(0.7)	82.7	(0.8)	81.4	(0.8)	95.1	(0.5)	71.7	(0.9)
Sub-national entities												
Abu Dhabi (United Arab Emirates)	93.1	(0.7)	96.5	(0.5)	93.4	(0.8)	93.2	(0.6)	96.6	(0.4)	95.1	(0.6)
Alberta (Canada)	82.2	(1.0)	91.1	(0.9)	84.7	(1.0)	86.1	(0.9)	94.3	(0.6)	84.0	(0.8)
England (United Kingdom)	81.4	(1.0)	93.3	(0.6)	86.3	(0.7)	90.2	(0.7)	96.7	(0.4)	84.6	(1.0)
Flanders (Belgium)	87.4	(0.7)	96.6	(0.4)	95.4	(0.5)	80.7	(1.1)	97.7	(0.3)	73.2	(1.1)
Average	80.3	(0.2)	89.4	(0.1)	84.8	(0.1)	81.9	(0.2)	92.0	(0.1)	77.4	(0.2)
United States	83.0	(1.0)	89.3	(1.1)	81.6	(1.4)	82.6	(1.0)	92.9	(0.7)	82.5	(0.9)

*See notes at the end of this chapter.
Source: OECD, TALIS 2013 Database.
StatLink http://dx.doi.org/10.1787/888933047463

The extent to which teachers across countries hold beliefs that are related to job satisfaction is shown in Figure 3.4 (OECD, 2014, Table 7.2). On average, 91% of teachers across countries reported overall satisfaction with their job, 93% of all teachers reported being satisfied with their performance in their current school, 84% would recommend their school as a good place to work, and 90% reported that they enjoy working at their current school. However, consistent with the findings for elements measuring self-efficacy, only 50% of teachers in Japan reported being satisfied with their performance in their current school, and 62% would recommend their school as a good place to work. Nevertheless, more than three-quarters (78%) of teachers in Japan reported that they enjoy working in their current school.

While an average of around 77% of teachers reported that the advantages of being a teacher clearly outweigh the disadvantages, in Brazil, the Czech Republic, France and the Slovak Republic, only 60% of teachers or less reported that they believe this.

Yet these results did not dissuade teachers in these four countries from reporting that they would choose to become a teacher if they had to make the decision again. Some 70% of teachers or more in these countries reported that if they had to decide again, they would still choose to work as a teacher (the TALIS average is 78%).

Figure 3.4
Teachers' job satisfaction
Percentage of lower secondary education teachers who "strongly disagree", "disagree", "agree" or "strongly agree" with the following statements

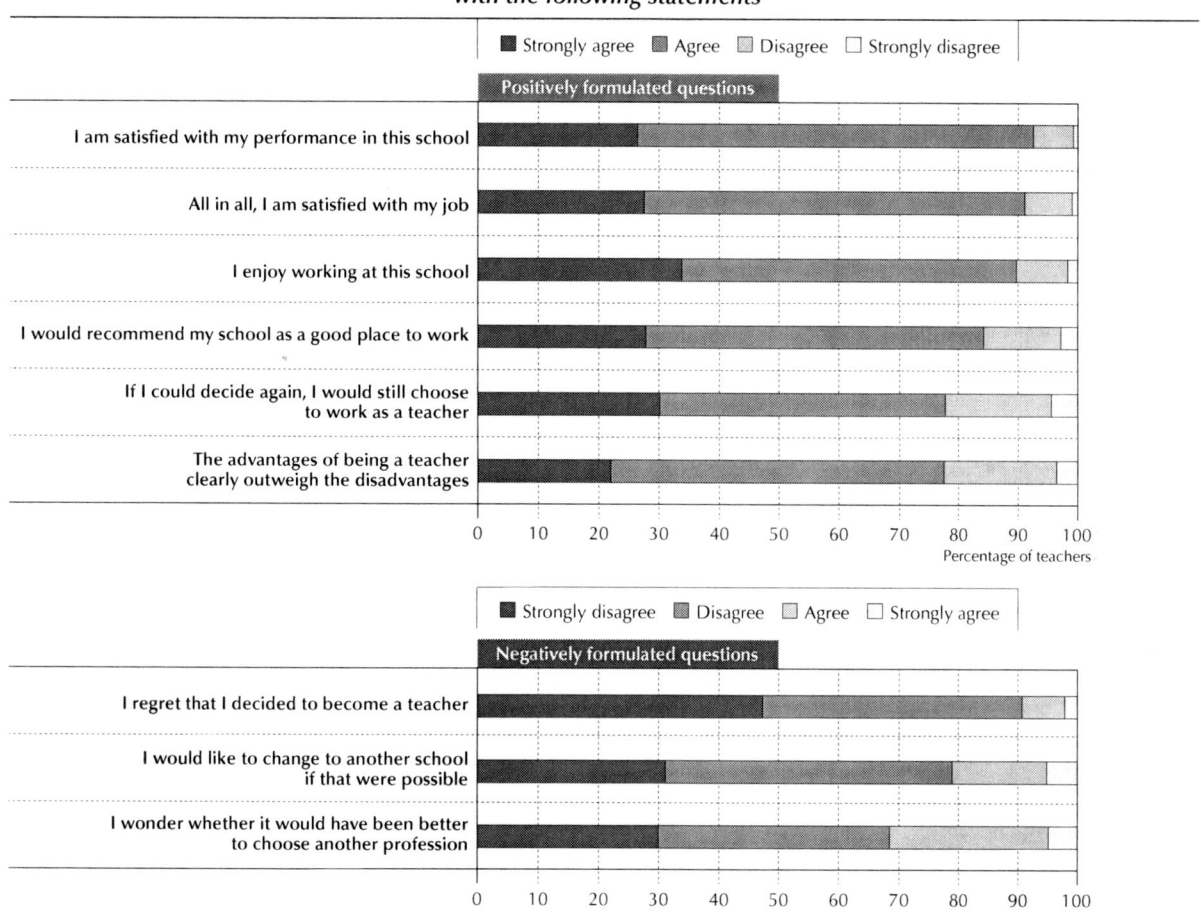

Positively formulated questions (Strongly agree, Agree, Disagree, Strongly disagree)
- I am satisfied with my performance in this school
- All in all, I am satisfied with my job
- I enjoy working at this school
- I would recommend my school as a good place to work
- If I could decide again, I would still choose to work as a teacher
- The advantages of being a teacher clearly outweigh the disadvantages

Negatively formulated questions (Strongly disagree, Disagree, Agree, Strongly agree)
- I regret that I decided to become a teacher
- I would like to change to another school if that were possible
- I wonder whether it would have been better to choose another profession

Items are ranked in descending order, based on the percentage of teachers who "strongly agree" or "agree" with the statement for positively formulated questions. For negatively formulated questions the order is reversed, meaning it is in descending order based on the percentage of teachers who "strongly disagree" or "disagree" with the statement.
Source: OECD, TALIS 2013 Database, Tables 7.2 and 7.2.Web.
StatLink http://dx.doi.org/10.1787/888933042200

As noted above, fewer than one in three teachers, on average across countries/economies, believes that teaching is a valued profession in society (Figure 3.2). This is a significant finding on its own, since even the perception of whether a profession is valued can affect the recruitment and retention of candidates in the profession. Large variations among the TALIS-participating countries and economies are observed, however. This perception is particularly pervasive among teachers in Croatia, France, the Slovak Republic, Spain and Sweden, where less than 10% of teachers believe that teaching is valued. In Korea, Malaysia, Singapore and Abu Dhabi (United Arab Emirates), however, the majority of teachers feels differently: at least two out of three teachers in these countries/economies reported that their society values teaching as a profession.

Additional analyses shed more light on the factors that might influence teachers' perceptions in this area.[2] The association with gender appears to be weak, as male teachers are more likely than female teachers to perceive teaching as a valued profession in only nine countries. Experience may play a role in shaping this belief: in 13 countries, teachers with more than five years of teaching experience perceive their profession to be less valued than do their less-experienced colleagues (OECD, 2014, Table 7.3).

Interestingly, in 28 of the countries and economies that participated in TALIS, the extent to which teachers can participate in decision making has a strong association with the likelihood of teachers reporting that they believe teaching is valued by society. In Bulgaria, Croatia and Latvia, when teachers are part of decision-making processes in their school, they were three times more likely to report that teaching is a valued profession in society, while teachers in Chile were more than five times more likely to do so.

Many countries have enacted policies aimed to increase the prestige of the teaching profession in order to avoid the deleterious effects of negative perceptions about teaching (Schleicher, 2011). Countries may want to conduct further analyses to look at the origins of these negative perceptions to identify what it is specifically about the teaching profession that engenders them.

TEACHERS' SELF-EFFICACY AND JOB SATISFACTION AS RELATED TO CLASSROOM ENVIRONMENT

Certain classroom characteristics can make a teacher's work more challenging. Teaching classes in which a large proportion of students have different achievement levels, special needs or behavioural problems can affect a teacher's self-efficacy and job satisfaction, especially if the teacher is not properly prepared or supported (Major, 2012). Most of the empirical evidence in this area comes from studies focused on teachers of students with special needs. TALIS finds that teaching special-needs students is one of the areas in which teachers reported that they need professional development the most. Other studies have shown that teachers of special-needs students tend to report less job satisfaction and poor self-efficacy, and have a greater chance of leaving their schools than do their colleagues who teach classes without such students. This is especially the case if they teach students with behavioural and emotional problems (Emery and Vandenberg, 2010; Katsiyannis et al., 2003). In addition, many of those who teach emotionally challenged children must also handle some degree of stress due to a lack of the specific skills and/or experience needed to teach children with these problems (Henderson et al., 2005).

This section investigates the associations between both teacher self-efficacy and job satisfaction, and class size and challenging classroom characteristics. Classrooms are considered to be challenging if more than 10% of students in the class are low achievers or more than 10% of students have behavioural problems.[3] Classrooms in which 10% or more of the students are academically gifted are also included in this category, as teaching to a wide range of student abilities in one class can also be a challenge (Major, 2012).

Figure 3.5
Teachers' job satisfaction and class composition

Teachers' job satisfaction level in lower secondary education according to the number of students in the classroom and according to the percentage of students with behavioural problems[1]

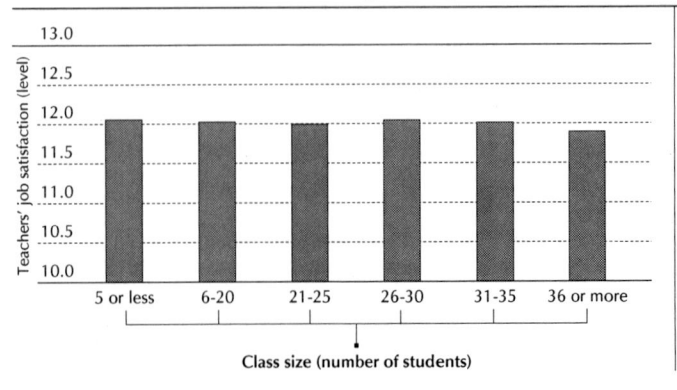

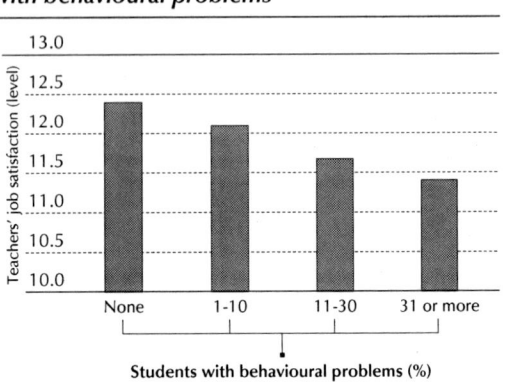

1. Data on class size and students with behavioural problems are reported by teachers and refer to a randomly chosen class they currently teach from their weekly timetable.
Source: OECD, TALIS 2013 Database.
StatLink http://dx.doi.org/10.1787/888933042276

Perhaps surprisingly, class size seems to have only a minimal effect on either teaching efficacy or job satisfaction, and in just a few countries (OECD, 2014, Tables 7.6 and 7.7). Other TALIS data indicate that it is not the number of students but the type of students who are in a class that has the largest association with the teacher's self-efficacy and job satisfaction. An example of this is provided in Figure 3.5, where the minimal effect of class size on teachers' job satisfaction is contrasted with the stronger influence of teaching students with behavioural problems.

The associations between challenging classroom characteristics and teachers' self-efficacy and job satisfaction tell an interesting story across TALIS-participating countries and economies. In many countries/economies, teachers teaching classes where more than one in ten students are low achievers or have behavioural problems reported significantly lower self-efficacy and less job satisfaction (OECD, 2014, Tables 7.6 and 7.7). The negative association between teaching more low achievers and self-efficacy is observed in only 9 countries, but the negative association between teaching these types of students and job satisfaction is observed in 24 countries. Teaching classes composed of more students with behavioural problems is associated with lower self-efficacy in 16 countries and with less job satisfaction in 29 countries. These associations with self-efficacy are at least moderately strong in 7 countries, while the associations with job satisfaction are at least moderately strong in 24 countries (OECD, 2014, Tables 7.6.Web and 7.7.Web). In contrast, teaching in classrooms where more than one in ten students is academically gifted is related to greater teacher self-efficacy in 17 countries and greater job satisfaction in 23 countries.

TEACHERS' SELF-EFFICACY AND THEIR RELATIONS WITH COLLEAGUES AND STUDENTS

Teachers' perceptions of school climate, the collaborative culture in school, and school leadership greatly affect their levels of stress, self-efficacy and job satisfaction (Collie et al., 2012; Demir, 2008). For example, stress due to students' behaviour has been found to be negatively related to teachers' self-efficacy, and stress related to workload and teachers' self-efficacy appears to be directly related to teachers' job satisfaction (Collie et al., 2012; Klassen and Chiu, 2010; Taylor and Tashakkori, 1994). These relationships are further reinforced by instructional leadership and by distributed leadership, which also serve to reduce teachers' sense of isolation and increase their commitment to the common good (Wahlstrom and Louis, 2008; Pounder, 1999).

Yet, even more important than principal leadership styles are the relationships teachers have with other teachers (in the TALIS questionnaire, this is measured by different ways of co-operating), their school leaders and their students (Louis, 2006). Next to teachers' sense of self-efficacy in their ability to manage their class (Box 3.1), having good relations with their colleagues and students seems to be the most crucial factor affecting teachers' job satisfaction and self-efficacy (Holzberger et al., 2013; Caprara et al., 2006; Klassen and Chiu, 2010).

In this section, teacher-leader relations are examined separately from teacher-teacher and teacher-student relations. Two aspects of the teacher-leader relationship are studied: the extent to which teachers are given opportunities to participate in decision making in their schools, and the instructional leadership that school principals provide (Box 3.2). The impact that these relationships can have on the associations between challenging classrooms and self-efficacy and job satisfaction is also discussed (OECD, 2014, Tables 7.6 and 7.7).

In all countries, when teachers reported more positive relationships with students and collaborative relationships with other teachers, they also reported significantly higher levels of self-efficacy (OECD, 2014, Table 7.8). The association appears to be stronger for teacher-teacher relations than for teacher-student relations in many countries.

Teacher-teacher collaborative relationships are also weakly-to-moderately associated with greater job satisfaction (OECD, 2014, Table 7.9), while teacher-student relations are strongly related to greater job satisfaction. In fact, in many cases, the teacher-student association is two to three times more strongly related to job satisfaction than the teacher-teacher relationship. In general, then, teachers' positive relationships with other teachers in the school seem to be particularly important for improving teachers' feelings of self-efficacy, while teachers' positive relationships with their students appear to have the greatest impact on their satisfaction with their job.

In 20 countries, teachers who agreed that the staff members at their school are given opportunities to participate in decision making reported greater self-efficacy (OECD, 2014, Table 7.8). An even more consistent and stronger relationship is observed between decision making at school and teachers' job satisfaction. The ability to participate in decision making at school is significantly related to a strong increase in teachers' job satisfaction across all countries (OECD, 2014, Table 7.9). Surprisingly, in contrast to the literature reviewed in this section, instructional leadership, as measured in TALIS, appears to be weakly associated with teachers' self-efficacy and job satisfaction.

Box 3.2. Description of in-school relationships

School leadership is measured with one item on distributed leadership and one index on instructional leadership. Teacher-student relations and teacher-teacher relations are measured with two indices, as outlined below.

Distributed leadership
- This school provides staff with opportunities to actively participate in school decisions.

Instructional leadership
- I took actions to support co-operation among teachers to develop new teaching practices.
- I took actions to ensure that teachers take responsibility for improving their teaching skills.
- I took actions to ensure that teachers feel responsible for their students' learning outcomes.

Teacher-student relationships
- In this school, teachers and students usually get on well with each other.
- Most teachers in this school believe that the students' well-being is important.
- Most teachers in this school are interested in what students have to say.
- If a student from this school needs extra assistance, the school provides it.

Teacher-teacher relationships
- Teach jointly as a team in the same class.
- Observe other teachers' classes and provide feedback.
- Engage in joint activities across different classes and age groups (e.g. projects).
- Exchange teaching materials with colleagues.
- Engage in discussions about the learning development of specific students.
- Work with other teachers in my school to ensure common standards in evaluations for assessing student progress.
- Attend team conferences.
- Take part in collaborative professional learning.

Source: OECD (2014), *TALIS 2013 Results: An International Perspective on Teaching and Learning*, http://dx.doi.org/10.1787/9789264196261-en.

How teachers' relationships with colleagues and students can moderate the influence of classroom composition

Good relations between teachers and their colleagues and between teachers and their students can mitigate the negative effects of challenging classrooms on teachers' self-efficacy and job satisfaction (OECD, 2014, Tables 7.6 and 7.7). Figure 3.6 illustrates the relationships that are discussed below.

Figure 3.6
The influence of class composition on teachers' attitudes and relationships

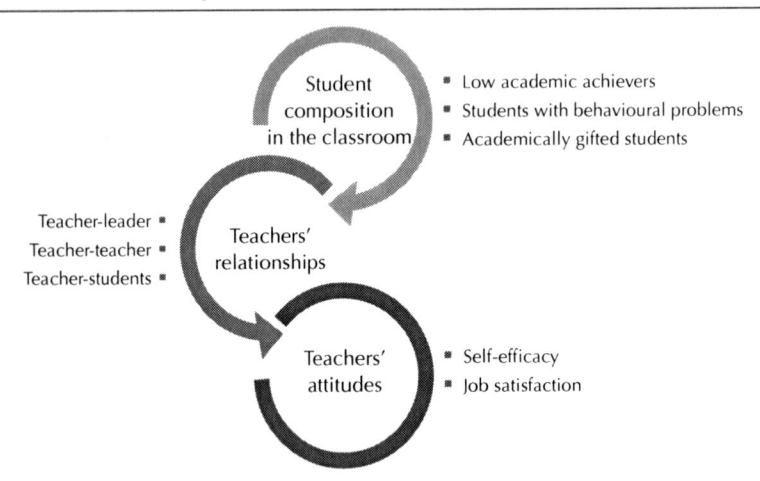

- Student composition in the classroom
  - Low academic achievers
  - Students with behavioural problems
  - Academically gifted students
- Teachers' relationships
  - Teacher-leader
  - Teacher-teacher
  - Teacher-students
- Teachers' attitudes
  - Self-efficacy
  - Job satisfaction

Source: OECD (2014), *TALIS 2013 Results: An International Perspective on Teaching and Learning*, http://dx.doi.org/10.1787/9789264196261-en.

The finding that teachers who work in classrooms where at least 10% of students are low achievers tended to report lower self-efficacy and less job satisfaction still holds after accounting for these in-school relationships; but in many countries, the association is weakened (see OECD, 2014, Tables 7.8.Web.1 and 7.9.Web.1 for teacher-student and teacher-teacher relationships, and OECD, 2014, Tables 7.8.Web.2 and 7.9.Web.2 for teacher-leader relationships, columns highlighted in light blue).[4]

When it comes to job satisfaction, the strength of the association is reduced in nearly all countries. In these cases, the relationships teachers have with their principal, their colleagues and their students can help to mitigate the adverse effects on self-efficacy and job satisfaction associated with working in classrooms with larger proportions of low-achieving students.

In general, teachers' in-school relationships do not seem to affect the strength of the associations between teaching classes with a large proportion of students with behavioural problems and teachers' self-efficacy. But in nearly all countries where teaching classes with a large proportion of students who misbehave was significantly associated with less job satisfaction, positive in-school relationships seem to reduce the strength of this association (OECD, 2014, Tables 7.8.Web.1, 7.8.Web.2, 7.9.Web.1 and 7.9.Web.2).

TEACHERS' SELF-EFFICACY AND THEIR PROFESSIONAL DEVELOPMENT

In summarising research on effective teacher professional development, Darling-Hammond and Richardson (2009) contend that successful programmes are sustained over time, are collaborative and focused on the content to be taught, and provide multiple opportunities for classroom application. Since teachers' beliefs, such as self-efficacy, are an important factor in facilitating student learning, they have recently become the target of professional development activities. Studies have shown that professional development activities that are focused on the three components of teachers' self-efficacy – classroom management, instruction and student engagement – strengthen teachers' beliefs in those areas as well as teachers' beliefs about student learning (Rosenfeld and Rosenfeld, 2008; Ross and Bruce, 2007a; Powell-Moman and Brown-Schild, 2011; Karimi, 2011).

Studies remain equivocal as to whether the duration of the professional development programme or teachers' years of work experience contribute to any impact that a professional development programme might have on teachers' self-efficacy and students' achievement (Lumpe et al., 2012; Wayne et al., 2008; Powell-Moman and Brown-Schild, 2011; Rosenfeld and Rosenfeld, 2008). When mentoring is considered, however, it seems that, especially for new teachers, time spent with a mentor, participation in mentor-facilitated professional development activities, and the quality of mentors' interactions are significantly related to teachers' self-efficacy and to the development of effective collaborative relationships (LoCasale-Crouch et al., 2012).

There are several types of professional development activities. There can be formally organised professional development activities, which could include induction programmes, mentoring programmes, classroom observations, workshops and conferences. There can also be more informally organised activities, which could also include a mentoring relationship in which a teacher can be either the mentor or the mentee in the relationship. This section examines the relationship between teachers' participation in different types and aspects of professional development, and their self-efficacy and job satisfaction.

In around one in four countries, teachers who reported that they have participated in mentoring activities also reported greater job satisfaction. In seven countries, teachers who reported that they were mentees reported greater job satisfaction, while in eight countries, being a mentor was related to greater job satisfaction (OECD, 2014, Table 7.11). The strength of the association between being a mentor and greater job satisfaction is moderate in six of these countries, and strong in Sweden.

In 14 countries/economies, participating in mentoring, observation or coaching programmes as part of a formal school arrangement is positively associated with self-efficacy. In seven countries, there is only a weak, albeit positive, relationship between this form of professional development and job satisfaction.

These findings suggest that being either a mentor or a mentee is associated with an improvement in teachers' job satisfaction, while these activities do not show a consistent association with teachers' self-efficacy across countries. Professional development activities that are part of a formal school arrangement are positively related to job satisfaction in only a few countries, although they relate positively to teachers' self-efficacy in twice as many countries.[5]

> **Box 3.3. Teacher development in Finland**
>
> In Finland, professional development for teachers is seen as a comprehensive process, which begins with initial teacher education. Teacher education has been available in universities since 1971, and a Master's degree is a requirement, including a Master's thesis. This kind of teacher education leads to teachers becoming reflective professionals who actively develop their own work and professional skills and methods, as researchers do, having had this research-based initial education.
>
> Finland does not have a nationally organised induction system. Education providers and individual schools have autonomy over arranging support for new teachers, and therefore there are notable differences between schools in ways of implementing induction. However, there is awareness of the increasing need for support for new teachers, and already many different applications of mentoring practices are in place. A specific model of peer-group mentoring has been developed and is being disseminated by the Finnish Network for Teacher Induction ("Osaava Verme"), which is part of a seven-year national Osaava programme (2010-16) funded by the Ministry of Education and Culture. The objective of the programme is to motivate education providers and individual institutions to take greater responsibility and a proactive approach to their own staff development activities with the help of networking activities and mutual co-operation.
>
> Source: Ministry of Education, Finland, 2014.

TEACHERS' SELF-EFFICACY AND THE APPRAISAL AND FEEDBACK THEY RECEIVE

Teacher appraisal and feedback can be used to recognise and celebrate teachers' strengths while simultaneously challenging teachers to address weaknesses in their pedagogical practices. Appraisal and feedback can have a significant impact on classroom instruction, teacher motivation and attitudes, as well as on student outcomes. Specifically, appraisal and feedback can play an important role in teachers' job satisfaction and self-efficacy. Although no research has directly investigated this yet, the impact of feedback and appraisal is expected to vary greatly, depending on the source. For example, while teachers say they derive little value from student ratings, teacher-solicited feedback is generally regarded as the most useful for improving teaching practices (Wininger and Birkholz, 2013; Ross and Bruce, 2007b; Michaelowa, 2002).

There are many methods and approaches that can be used to appraise and provide feedback to teachers. It is important to look at whether teachers receive feedback from more than one appraiser and the types of feedback they receive, such as results from student surveys or students' test scores, or feedback on classroom management. Teachers' perceptions of the impact of the appraisal are also relevant. For example, do teachers regard appraisals as having a concrete impact on their teaching or as simply an administrative exercise? Box 3.4 explains how the TALIS questionnaire items on appraisal and feedback were compressed into the six measures discussed in this section.

> **Box 3.4. Appraisal and feedback measures**
>
> Six measures of appraisal and feedback are used:
>
> **Number of evaluators**
> The first measure identifies whether teachers were appraised by more than one evaluator.
>
> **Types of feedback**
> The next three measures identify the types, or sources, of feedback teachers received. Teachers' responses were categorised according to whether they reported that the feedback they received considered the following three elements to be of moderate or high importance:
> - student surveys
> - students' test scores
> - feedback on their classroom management of student behaviour
>
> **Teachers' perceptions of appraisal and feedback**
> The last two measures concern teachers' perceptions related to their appraisal and feedback. The first measure relates to teachers' responses about the extent to which they agreed that their appraisal affected their teaching. The second measure concerns the extent to which teachers agreed that their appraisal was performed primarily for administrative purposes.
>
> Source: OECD (2014), TALIS 2013 Results: An International Perspective on Teaching and Learning, http://dx.doi.org/10.1787/9789264196261-en.

In 13 of the participating countries/economies, teachers who reported having at least two evaluators also reported greater self-efficacy (OECD, 2014, Table 7.12). In 23 countries, teachers who reported having at least two evaluators also reported greater job satisfaction (OECD, 2014, Table 7.13). The association is weak-to-moderate in most cases. Receiving feedback from student surveys is associated with greater self-efficacy in almost all TALIS-participating countries and economies, and with job satisfaction in 20 countries. These findings could be interpreted in two ways. Teachers might receive feedback from student surveys that helps them to feel more confident in their abilities and more satisfied with their jobs. Alternatively, it might be that the teachers who are more confident and content with their roles are those who conduct student surveys in the first place.

Box 3.5. The use of teacher and student feedback in Norway

Following several years of collaboration, the Norwegian Student Organisation and the Union of Education Norway have developed a number of recommendations for teacher appraisal. The purpose of their collaboration was to develop a set of agreed principles that can form the basis for a student survey on teaching in particular classes, with the possibility of adapting it locally. Following their recommendations, the survey should:

- Focus on teaching practice rather than the teacher as an individual.
- Include the students' own self-assessment and assessment of peers to enable analysis of how student effort and motivation influence the learning environment.
- Feature questions on teaching approaches that are relevant for student learning, such as adapted education and feedback to students, as well as questions on the general framework for teaching, such as materials and physical conditions.
- Be carried out anonymously to ensure that students give honest answers.
- Be analysed by the teacher and students together with a view to improve the classroom environment and learning outcomes.

This should be followed up with a joint report by the teacher and student group on their analysis of results and agreed future changes. This report, together with relevant data, should be submitted to the teachers' closest supervisor.

Source: Norwegian Directorate for Education and Training (2011), cited in Nusche, et al. (2011), *OECD Reviews of Evaluation and Assessment in Education: Norway 2011*, http://dx.doi.org/10.1787/9789264117006-en.

In 24 countries, teachers who receive feedback from student test scores reported greater self-efficacy (OECD, 2014, Table 7.12). This type of feedback is also related to greater job satisfaction in 17 participating countries/economies (OECD, 2014, Table 7.13). Receiving feedback on classroom management is positively related to self-efficacy in 17 participating countries. In 23 countries, teachers who receive feedback on classroom management also reported greater job satisfaction; and in half of these countries, the association is strong.

In 10 participating countries and economies, teachers who reported that feedback affects their teaching also reported greater self-efficacy (OECD, 2014, Table 7.12). The perception that appraisal and feedback influences teaching practices is also positively related to job satisfaction in nearly all countries and economies surveyed (OECD, 2014, Table 7.13). In contrast, in 14 countries/economies, when teachers regarded their appraisal and feedback as only an administrative exercise, they tended to report lower self-efficacy; in all participating countries/economies, teachers who regarded appraisal and feedback in this way reported less job satisfaction. This negative association with job satisfaction is strong in most countries; only in Brazil is it weak.

TEACHERS' SELF-EFFICACY AND THEIR BELIEFS AND PRACTICES

To equip students with the skills and competencies needed in the 21st century, teachers around the world are being encouraged to use a variety of teaching practices, ranging from more traditional practices (such as direct transmission of information), to more recently conceived, constructivist practices. The latter forms of teaching and learning help to develop students' skills to manage complex situations and learn both independently and continuously. It has also been argued that these practices enhance students' motivation and achievement (Nie and Lau, 2010; Guthrie et al., 2000; Hacker and Tenent, 2002; Nie et al., 2013). Research advocating constructivist approaches also suggests that teachers' self-efficacy is greater among those teachers who use constructivist instruction techniques than among those who use reception or direct transmission instruction techniques (Luke et al., 2005; Nie et al., 2013). Using TALIS 2008 data, Vieluf et al. (2012) reported that the impact of direct transmission versus constructivist approaches depends on different factors, such as the subjects taught and classroom variables. In fact, it was not the use of one kind of practice rather than another, per se, but the variety of practices employed that was found to be related to greater teacher self-efficacy, among other things.

TALIS data indicate that, in most countries, constructivist beliefs are positively related to greater self-efficacy and job satisfaction among teachers (OECD, 2014, Tables 7.14 and 7.15). Teachers who reported more highly constructivist beliefs also reported greater self-efficacy and slightly more job satisfaction.

The number of hours spent teaching in a typical work week is more strongly associated with teachers' self-efficacy than with job satisfaction – although in opposite ways. All of these associations are weak (OECD, 2014, Tables 7.14.Web.2 and 7.15.Web.2).

In almost all countries/economies, the more time teachers spend on keeping order in the classroom, the less self-efficacy and less job satisfaction they reported. Meanwhile, the proportion of time spent on administrative tasks in the classroom seems to be weakly and negatively associated with job satisfaction in about half of the countries surveyed, while it relates negatively to self-efficacy in 12 countries (OECD, 2014, Tables 7.14.Web.4 and 7.15.Web.4).

How teachers' beliefs and practices mediate the impact of classroom composition on their sense of self-efficacy and job satisfaction

The proportion of time spent keeping order in the classroom plays the most crucial role in the relationships between classroom composition and teachers' self-efficacy and job satisfaction (OECD, 2014, Table 7.14.Web.3). Among teachers who teach larger proportions of low achievers and who reported less self-efficacy, the proportion of time these teachers reported spending on keeping order in the classroom accounts fully for that negative association in Italy, Serbia, Spain and Sweden, and reduces the strength of that association in Brazil, France, Mexico, Portugal and Romania. In other words, it is not that these teachers teach in classrooms with more low achievers that is related to their lower levels of self-efficacy; rather, it is the larger proportion of time that they spend on keeping order in the classroom that undermines their feelings of self-efficacy.

Figure 3.7

The influence of class composition on teachers' attitudes, beliefs and practices

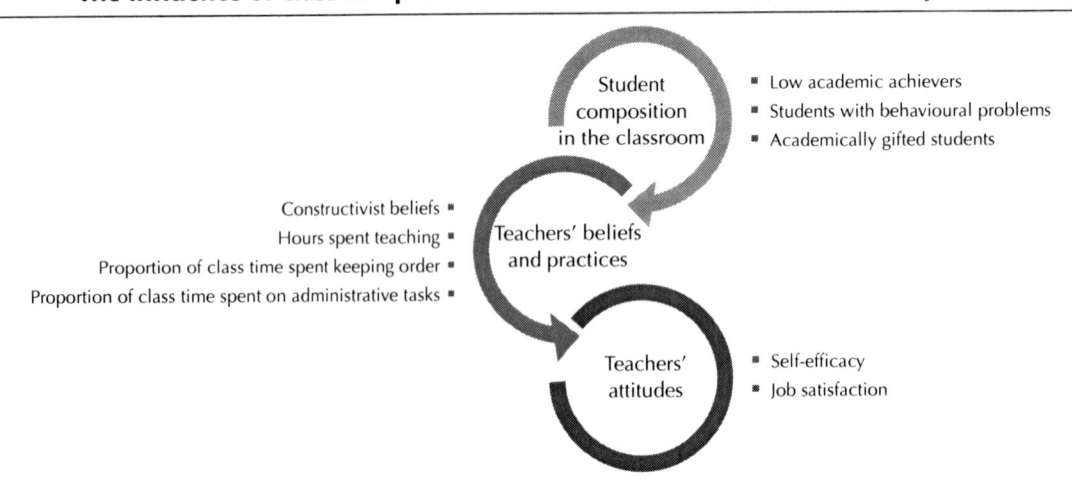

Student composition in the classroom
- Low academic achievers
- Students with behavioural problems
- Academically gifted students

Teachers' beliefs and practices
- Constructivist beliefs
- Hours spent teaching
- Proportion of class time spent keeping order
- Proportion of class time spent on administrative tasks

Teachers' attitudes
- Self-efficacy
- Job satisfaction

Source: OECD (2014), *TALIS 2013 Results: An International Perspective on Teaching and Learning*, http://dx.doi.org/10.1787/9789264196261-en.

A similar finding emerges among teachers who work in classrooms with larger proportions of students with behavioural problems and who reported lower levels of self-efficacy. The proportion of time these teachers spend keeping order in the classroom accounts fully for this negative association in ten countries; in Poland, Romania and Abu Dhabi (United Arab Emirates), the association is weakened after considering the proportion of time spent keeping order in class. What this means is that, in many countries, the relationship between teaching in challenging classrooms (i.e. classrooms containing more low achievers or students with behavioural problems) and teacher self-efficacy can be explained by the amount of time that a teacher spends keeping order in the class (OECD, 2014, Table 7.15.Web.3).

TEACHERS' SELF-EFFICACY AND THEIR PROFESSIONAL COLLABORATIVE PRACTICES

Formal collaborative learning generally entails teachers meeting regularly to share responsibility for their students' success at school (Chong and Kong, 2012). Although an increasing number of professional development activities for teachers are structured around collaboration, evidence on conditions for successful collaboration and positive outcomes related to collaborative practices remains relatively scarce and inconclusive (Nelson et al., 2008). Yet researchers have described a myriad of different structures and processes to create a collaborative culture among teachers in schools (Erickson et al., 2005; Nelson et al., 2008).

Empirical evidence shows that collaboration among teachers may enhance their efficacy, which, in turn, may improve student achievement and sustain positive teacher behaviours (Liaw, 2009; Puchner and Taylor, 2006). In a meta-review of empirical studies, Cordingley et al. (2003) reported that collaborative professional development is related to a positive impact on teachers' range of teaching practices and instructional strategies, to their ability to match these to their students' needs, and to their self-esteem and self-efficacy. There is also evidence that such collaborative professional development activities are linked to a positive influence on student learning processes, motivation and outcomes.

Box 3.6. Collaborative evaluation in Denmark

In Denmark, teacher appraisal is not regulated by law and no national requirements exist to evaluate the performance of teachers. Actual teacher-appraisal practices are determined locally with the possible influence of municipal requirements or guidelines. According to the *Folkeskole* Act, the school principal is responsible for the quality of teaching at the school as well as the overall administrative and pedagogical management of the school, including the professional development of teachers. As a result, the main responsibility for designing, introducing and organising teacher-appraisal procedures within the school lies with the school principal. Actual teacher-appraisal practices in Danish schools seem to be based on a culture where school leaders show confidence in their teachers, appraisal is conducted as a school-teacher or teacher-teacher dialogue, and procedures are defined in collaboration with the teachers.

Work in Danish schools is increasingly organised in a way that encourages teamwork. Schools are increasingly structuring work around teams of teachers (e.g. class team, form team, section team, subject team) that share responsibility for organising their work. This development has led to growing co-operation among teachers and a more formal dialogue between the school leaders and teams of teachers. This also provides a context in which some schools organise teacher appraisal mostly within teams. In this situation, teachers co-operate on promoting the quality of the teaching in the school. It is a widespread practice in the *Folkeskole* that planning, learning and knowledge sharing take place in teacher teams. Other typical activities among teachers include supervising each other within a team and discussing together the progress and development of an individual student. According to the *Folkeskole* Act, the school leader is responsible for the quality in his/her school within the limits imposed by the decisions of the city council and the school board.

Source: Shewbride, C. et al. (2011), *OECD Reviews of Evaluation and Assessment in Education: Denmark 2011*, http://dx.doi.org/10.1787/9789264116597-en.

TALIS examines the associations between several collaborative practices and teacher self-efficacy and job satisfaction. Specifically, the following indicators for collaborative practices were used: teaching jointly in the same class; observing and providing feedback on other teachers' classes; engaging in joint activities across different classes and age groups; and taking part in collaborative professional learning. Teachers who reported that they engage in these kinds of activities five times a year or more are compared with those who reported engaging in them less frequently.

In almost all countries, teachers who reported that they engage in these kinds of collaborative activities five times a year or more also reported greater self-efficacy. In half of the countries, this relationship is moderately strong (OECD, 2014, Table 7.16). Particularly strong associations are observed in Bulgaria, Chile, Estonia, Finland, Israel and Korea.

Similar to the results for teacher self-efficacy, almost all countries showed a positive relationship between teacher collaboration and job satisfaction (OECD, 2014, Table 7.17). Some relationships are particularly strong. For example, teachers in Chile and Estonia who jointly teach classes with other teachers reported greater job satisfaction (OECD, 2014, Table 7.17.Web). In eight countries, teachers who observe other teachers' classes also reported greater job satisfaction.

Chapter 3 — Strengthening teachers' confidence in their own abilities

This association is moderately strong in these countries. The strongest association with teachers' job satisfaction appears to be participating in collaborative professional learning activities five times a year or more. In two-thirds of the countries/economies surveyed, such participation is related to significantly greater job satisfaction. Of these, 12 countries show moderately strong associations; in Brazil and Chile exceptionally strong associations are observed. This means that teachers who take part in collaborative learning activities more frequently also reported much greater job satisfaction than those who do not.

Box 3.7. Preparing teachers to lead improvement in Japan

The Japanese tradition of lesson study, in which groups of teachers review their lessons and how to improve them, in part by analysing student errors, provides one of the most effective mechanisms for teachers' self-reflection as well as being a tool for continuous improvement. Observers of Japanese elementary school classrooms have long noted the consistency and thoroughness with which a math concept is taught and the way in which the teacher leads a discussion of mathematical ideas, both correct and incorrect, so that students gain a firm grasp on the concept. This school-by-school lesson study often culminates in large public research lessons. For example, when a new subject is added to the national curriculum, groups of teachers and researchers review research and curriculum materials and refine their ideas in pilot classrooms over a year before holding a public research lesson, which can be viewed electronically by hundreds of teachers, researchers and policy makers.

The tradition of lesson study in Japan also means that Japanese teachers are not alone. They work together in a disciplined way to improve the quality of the lessons they teach. That means that teachers whose practice lags behind that of the leaders can see what good practice is. Because their colleagues know who the poor performers are and discuss them, the poor performers have both the incentive and the means to improve their performance. Since the structure of the East Asian teaching workforce includes opportunities to become a master teacher and move up a ladder of increasing prestige and responsibility, it also pays for the good teacher to become even better.

Source: OECD (2011), *Strong Performers and Successful Reformers in Education: Lessons from PISA for the United States*, http://dx.doi.org/10.1787/9789264096660-en.

The relationships between collaborative practices and teachers' self-efficacy and job satisfaction, on average across countries, are illustrated in Figures 3.8 and 3.9, respectively. When looking at all TALIS countries and economies, the more frequent the participation in collaborative practices, the greater the teachers' sense of self-efficacy.

Figure 3.8

Teachers' self-efficacy and professional collaboration

Teachers' self-efficacy level according to the frequency of teacher professional collaboration for the following items for lower secondary education teachers

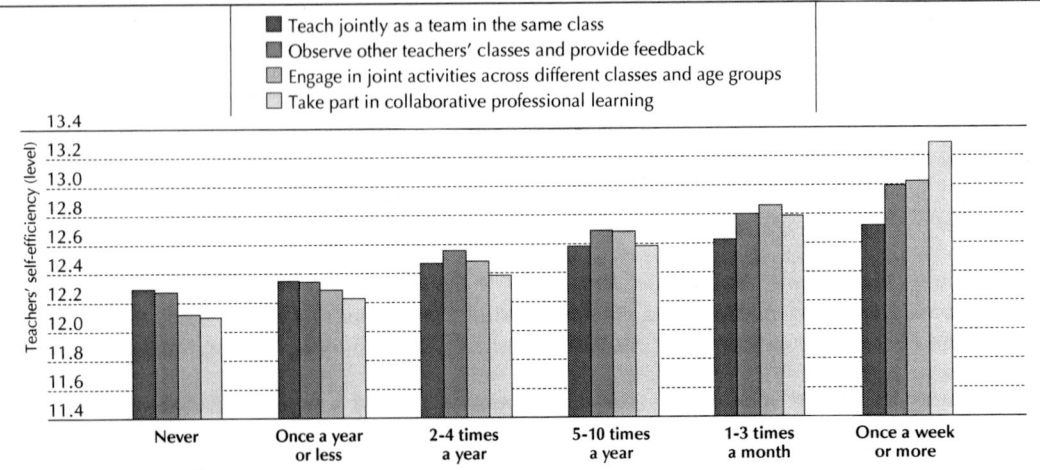

- Teach jointly as a team in the same class
- Observe other teachers' classes and provide feedback
- Engage in joint activities across different classes and age groups
- Take part in collaborative professional learning

Source: OECD, TALIS 2013 Database.
StatLink http://dx.doi.org/10.1787/888933042295

Strengthening teachers' confidence in their own abilities · Chapter 3

Figure 3.9
Teachers' job satisfaction and professional collaboration
Teachers' job satisfaction level according to the frequency of teacher professional collaboration for the following items for lower secondary education teachers

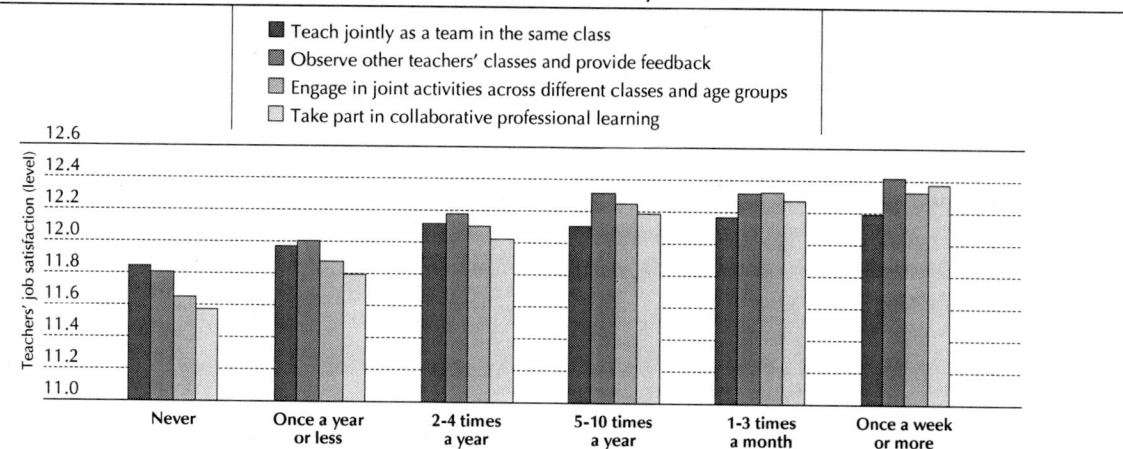

- Teach jointly as a team in the same class
- Observe other teachers' classes and provide feedback
- Engage in joint activities across different classes and age groups
- Take part in collaborative professional learning

Source: OECD, TALIS 2013 Database.
StatLink http://dx.doi.org/10.1787/888933042314

The strength of the association with job satisfaction appears to level off as teachers participate more frequently in collaborative activities. In general, however, more frequent engagement in collaborative practices seems to be associated with greater self-efficacy and job satisfaction among teachers across all the countries and economies that participated in TALIS.

POLICY IMPLICATIONS

The concepts of teacher self-efficacy and job satisfaction are more important to schools and education systems than a superficial reading might indicate. In other words, it is not just about making sure that teachers are happy and feel good about themselves and their teaching, although, of course, that is important as well. Research cited here suggests that there are positive associations between both self-efficacy and job satisfaction and student achievement. High levels of teacher self-efficacy are also associated with student motivation and other positive teacher behaviours. Conversely, low levels of self-efficacy can be linked to greater stress and problems dealing with students who misbehave. TALIS data also demonstrate that, in most countries, improving teachers' sense of self-efficacy is slightly more likely to result in greater job satisfaction than the other way around. Job satisfaction is important in itself as it relates to teachers' level of commitment to the profession and, in turn, to schools' ability to retain the best teachers.

As reported above, nine out of ten teachers are satisfied with their jobs, and 70%-92% of teachers are confident in their abilities in the areas measured. The biggest differences come at the country level. Differences in reported levels of efficacy and job satisfaction come from a variety of sources, depending on the country; but across countries/economies, challenging classrooms play a large role. This is hardly a surprise given the amount of time a teacher spends in his or her classroom and the importance of the work that is done – or should be done – there. If a teacher spends an inordinate amount of time keeping order, or if a larger proportion of his or her students misbehaves, it is natural to think that this teacher might feel less confident in his or her abilities or feel less positive about his or her job. The TALIS data support this.

Fortunately, TALIS data also identify the positive influences on teachers' sense of self-efficacy and job satisfaction that can aid in policy or programme development in these areas. A new report based on TALIS data (Burns and Darling-Hammond, 2014) also suggests policies that can support and strengthen teaching and lead to high-quality learning for students.

Build teachers' capacity to handle misbehaving students

TALIS data indicate that as the proportion of students with behavioural problems grows, teachers report less job satisfaction. In addition, in most countries/economies, teachers who spend more time keeping order in the classroom reported lower levels of self-efficacy and job satisfaction. When these relationships are examined further, the analyses finds that these negative relationships between both self-efficacy and job satisfaction and specific classroom factors can also be elucidated by a teacher's reports of how much time he or she spends keeping order in class. In other words, it is not the proportion of students with behavioural problems or low achievers in a class that is the most important influence on a teacher's self-efficacy or job satisfaction. Rather, it is the time the teacher spends dealing with the classroom-management issues related to these, or other, students.

Though it is impossible to identify cause and effect, the analyses reported here make a case for building teacher capacity so that the impact of students' behavioural problems on teaching and learning can be mitigated. This could benefit not only the teacher but also all of the students in the class. Professional development activities that focus on classroom management or instruction strategies might be useful, particularly for newer teachers, as would be providing additional classroom or pedagogical support for teachers who teach particularly challenging classes. It is equally important to be sure that during initial teacher education, teachers have several sufficiently long periods of teaching practice in a variety of schools to ensure that beginning teachers do not enter the profession until they have developed adequate classroom competencies. More flexible classroom situations, such as team teaching, might also allow teachers to share the tasks of teaching and disciplining students.

Support the development of interpersonal relationships within the school

TALIS shows that the interpersonal relationships in a school have powerful mediating effects on some of the challenging classroom circumstances that teachers might face. In addition, the relationships that teachers have with their students have a strong association with teachers' job satisfaction.

School leaders need to provide opportunities and support for building these relationships at school. The support could be in the form of resources, such as a physical space in which teachers can meet with each other, or time away from class or other administrative work to allow teachers to meet and develop relationships with students and colleagues. The leadership team needs to make itself available to its teaching staff as well. Government policies can also offer school leaders the organisational freedom to develop strategies in these areas and to make changes in the school day or school building to help. Perhaps most important, teachers need to be open and willing to engage with their colleagues, their administration and their students.

Institute meaningful systems of appraisal and feedback that have connections with teachers' practice

In all TALIS-participating countries and economies, teachers' perception that appraisal and feedback lead to changes in their teaching practice is related to greater job satisfaction, while their perception that appraisal and feedback are only administrative exercises is related to less job satisfaction.

Policy makers and schools should thus support the development of teacher appraisal and feedback systems that are actually linked to improving teaching.

Encourage collaboration among teachers, either through professional development activities or classroom practices

Collaboration among teachers is important not just for building the interpersonal relationships among staff that are shown have an impact on teachers' self-efficacy and job satisfaction, but because they are valuable in and of themselves. It is clear from the TALIS data that teachers benefit from even minimal amounts of collaboration with colleagues. The data show that participating in collaborative professional development activities or engaging in collaborative practices five times a year or more has a positive relationship with both teacher self-efficacy and job satisfaction. Many of the collaborative practices mentioned in TALIS, such as observing other teachers' classes and providing feedback, or teaching as a team in the same class, could – and should – be introduced at school. These activities serve a variety of purposes, including providing professional development for teachers where they work and offering teachers another source of feedback on their work. School leaders could make schedules more flexible to allow for team teaching, for example.

Notes

1. Teachers responded that they could perform these actions "quite a bit" or "a lot", which has here been summarised as "often".

2. These analyses were made up of binary logistic regressions conducted for each country separately. The combined Strongly Disagree-Disagree group was chosen as a reference category for the analysis examining the extent to which teachers feel that teaching is a valued profession in society.

3. Similarly, the cut-off points were determined by reviewing the distribution of responses and selecting a point where both representation of the responses and sufficient variability to be meaningful were maintained.

4. Note that the baseline classroom composition coefficients used in OECD, 2014, Tables 7.8 to 7.15 are slightly different from those presented in OECD, 2014, Tables 7.6 and 7.7. This is due to differences in the analyses performed.

5. In supplementary analyses (not discussed here), there does not appear to be consistent or significant changes in classroom composition correlations with self-efficacy or job satisfaction after accounting for professional development.

Notes regarding Cyprus

Note by Turkey: The information in this document with reference to "Cyprus" relates to the southern part of the Island. There is no single authority representing both Turkish and Greek Cypriot people on the Island. Turkey recognises the Turkish Republic of Northern Cyprus (TRNC). Until a lasting and equitable solution is found within the context of the United Nations, Turkey shall preserve its position concerning the "Cyprus issue".

Note by all the European Union Member States of the OECD and the European Union: The Republic of Cyprus is recognised by all members of the United Nations with the exception of Turkey. The information in this document relates to the area under the effective control of the Government of the Republic of Cyprus.

Note regarding Israel

The statistical data for Israel are supplied by and under the responsibility of the relevant Israeli authorities. The use of such data by the OECD is without prejudice to the status of the Golan Heights, East Jerusalem and Israeli settlements in the West Bank under the terms of international law.

Note regarding the United States

The data from the United States are located below the line in selected tables in this report and are not included in the calculations for the international average. This is because the United States did not meet the international standards for participation rates. See Annex A of OECD (2014), *TALIS 2013 Results: An International Perspective on Teaching and Learning*.

References

Burns, D. and L. Darling-Hammond (2014), *Teaching Around the World: What Can TALIS Tell Us?*, Stanford Center for Opportunity Policy in Education, Stanford.

Caprara, G.V. et al. (2006), "Teachers' self-efficacy beliefs as determinants of job satisfaction and students' academic achievement: A study at the school level", *Journal of School Psychology*, Vol. 44/6, pp. 473-490.

Caprara, G.V. et al. (2003), "Efficacy beliefs as determinants of teachers' job satisfaction", *Journal of Educational Psychology*, Vol. 95/4, pp. 821-832.

Chong, W.H. and C.A. Kong (2012), "Teacher collaborative learning and teacher self-efficacy: The case of lesson study", *Journal of Experimental Education*, Vol. 80/3, pp. 263-283.

Collie, R.J., J.D. Shapka and N.E. Perry (2012), "School climate and socio-emotional learning: Predicting teacher stress, job satisfaction, and teaching efficacy", *Journal of Educational Psychology*, Vol. 104/4, pp. 1189-1204.

Cordingley P. et al. (2003), "The impact of collaborative CPD on classroom teaching and learning", in *Research Evidence in Education Library*, EPPI-Centre, Social Science Research Unit, Institute of Education, University of London, London.

Darling-Hammond, L. and N. Richardson (2009), "Teacher learning: What matters?", *Educational Leadership*, Vol. 66/5, pp. 46-53.

Demir, K. (2008), "Transformational leadership and collective efficacy: The moderating roles of collaborative culture and teachers' self-efficacy", *Egitim, Arastirmalari – Eurasian Journal of Educational Research*, Vol. 33, pp. 93-112.

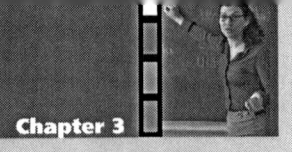

Emery, D.W. and B. Vandenberg (2010), "Special education teacher burnout and ACT", *International Journal of Special Education*, Vol. 25/3, pp. 119-131.

Erickson, G. et al. (2005), "Collaborative teacher learning: Findings from two professional development projects", *Teacher and Teacher Education*, Vol. 21, pp. 787-798.

Guthrie, J.T., A. Wigfield and C. VonSecker (2000), "Effects of integrated instruction on motivation and strategy use in reading", *Journal of Educational Psychology*, Vol. 92, pp. 331-341.

Hacker, D.J. and A. Tenent (2002), "Implementing reciprocal teaching in the classroom: Overcoming obstacles and making modifications", *Journal of Educational Psychology*, Vol. 94, pp. 699-718.

Henderson, K. et al. (2005), "Teachers of children with emotional disturbance: A national look at preparation, teaching conditions, and practices", *Behavioral Disorders*, Vol. 31/1, pp. 6-17.

Holzberger, D., A. Philipp and M. Kunter (2013), "How teachers' self-efficacy is related to instructional quality: A longitudinal analysis", *Journal of Educational Psychology*, online first publication, April 29, 2013, http://dx.doi.org/10.1037/a0032198.

Karimi, M.N. (2011), "The effects of professional development initiatives on EFL teachers' degree of self-efficacy", *Australian Journal of Teacher Education*, Vol. 36/6, pp. 50-62.

Katsiyannis, A., D. Zhang and M.A. Conroy (2003), "Availability of special education teachers", *Remedial and Special Education*, Vol. 24/4, pp. 246-253.

Klassen, R.M. and M.M. Chiu (2010), "Effect on teachers' self-efficacy and job satisfaction: Teacher gender, years of experience, and job stress", *Journal of Educational Psychology*, Vol. 102/3, pp. 741-756.

Liaw, E.C. (2009), "Teacher efficacy of pre-service teachers in Taiwan: The influence of classroom teaching and group discussions", *Teaching and Teacher Education*, Vol. 25, pp. 176-180.

LoCasale-Crouch, J. et al. (2012), "The role of the mentor in supporting new teachers: Associations with self-efficacy, reflection, and quality", *Mentoring and Tutoring: Partnership in Learning*, Vol. 20/3, pp. 303-323.

Louis, K.S. (2006), "Changing the culture of schools: Professional community, organizational learning, and trust", *Journal of School Leadership*, Vol. 16, pp. 477-487.

Luke, A. et al. (2005), *Innovation and Enterprise in Classroom Practice: A Discussion of Enabling and Disenabling Pedagogical Factors in P5 and S3 Classrooms*, Centre for Research in Instruction and Practice, Singapore.

Lumpe, A. et al. (2012), "Beliefs about teaching science: The relationship between elementary teachers' participation in professional development and student achievement", *International Journal of Science Education*, Vol. 34/2, pp. 153-166.

Major, A.E. (2012), "Job design for special education teachers", *Current Issues in Education*, Vol. 15/2, http://cie.asu.edu/ojs/index.php/cieatasu/article/view/900/333.

Michaelowa, K. (2002), *Teacher Job Satisfaction, Student Achievement, and the Cost of Primary Education in Francophone Sub-Saharan Africa*, Hamburg Institute of International Economics.

Nelson, T.H. et al. (2008), "A culture of collaborative inquiry: Learning to develop and support professional learning communities", *Teachers College Record*, Vol. 110, pp. 1269-1303.

Nie, Y. et al. (2013), "The roles of teacher efficacy in instructional innovation: Its predictive relations to constructivist and didactic instruction", *Educational Research for Policy and Practice*, Vol. 12/1, pp. 67-77.

Nie, Y. and S. Lau (2010), "Differential relations of traditional and constructivist instruction to students' cognition, motivation, and achievement", *Learning and Instruction*, Vol. 20, pp. 411-423.

Nusche, D. et al. (2011), *OECD Reviews of Evaluation and Assessment in Education: Norway 2011*, OECD Reviews of Evaluation and Assessment in Education, OECD Publishing, Paris, http://dx.doi.org/10.1787/9789264117006-en.

OECD (2014), *TALIS 2013 Results: An International Perspective on Teaching and Learning*, OECD Publishing, Paris, http://dx.doi.org/10.1787/9789264196261-en.

OECD (2011), *Strong Performers and Successful Reformers in Education: Lessons from PISA for the United States*, OECD Publishing, Paris, http://dx.doi.org/10.1787/9789264096660-en.

Pounder, D.G. (1999), "Teacher teams: Exploring job characteristics and work-related outcomes of work group enhancement", *Educational Administration Quarterly*, Vol. 35/3, pp. 317-348.

Powell-Moman, A.D. and V.B. Brown-Schild (2011), "The influence of a two-year professional development institute on teacher self-efficacy and use of inquiry-based instruction", *Science Educator*, Vol. 20/2, pp. 47-53.

Puchner, L.D. and A.R. Taylor (2006), "Lesson study, collaboration and teacher efficacy: Stories from two-school based math lesson study groups", *Teaching and Teacher Education*, Vol. 22, pp. 922-934.

Rosenfeld, M. and S. Rosenfeld (2008), "Developing effective teacher beliefs about learners: The role of sensitizing teachers to individual learning differences", *Educational Psychology*, Vol. 28/3, pp. 245-272.

Ross, J. and C. Bruce (2007a), "Professional development effects on teacher efficacy: Results of a randomized field trial", *Journal of Educational Research*, Vol. 101/1, pp. 50-60.

Ross, J. and C. Bruce (2007b), "Teacher self-assessment: A mechanism for facilitating professional growth", *Teaching and Teacher Education*, Vol. 23, pp. 146-159.

Schleicher, A. (2011), *Building a High-Quality Teaching Profession: Lessons from around the World*, OECD Publishing, Paris, http://dx.doi.org/10.1787/9789264113046-en.

Shewbride, C. et al. (2011), *OECD Reviews of Evaluation and Assessment in Education: Denmark 2011*, OECD Reviews of Evaluation and Assessment in Education, OECD Publishing, Paris, http://dx.doi.org/10.1787/9789264116597-en.

Skaalvik, E.M. and S. Skaalvik (2007), "Dimensions of teacher self-efficacy and relations with strain factors, perceived collective teacher efficacy, and teacher burnout", *Journal of Educational Psychology*, Vol. 99/3, pp. 611-625.

Taylor, D.L. and A. Tashakkori (1994), "Predicting teachers' sense of efficacy and job satisfaction using school climate and participatory decision making", presented at the Annual Meeting of the Southwest Educational Research Association, January 1994, San Antonio, TX.

Tschannen-Moran, M. and M. Barr (2004), "Fostering student achievement: The relationship between collective teacher efficacy and student achievement", *Leadership and Policy in Schools*, Vol. 3/3, pp. 187-207.

Tschannen-Moran, M. and A. Woolfolk Hoy (2001), "Teacher efficacy: Capturing an elusive construct", *Teaching and Teacher Education*, Vol. 17/7, pp. 783-805.

Vieluf, S. et al. (2012), *Teaching Practices and Pedagogical Innovation: Evidence from TALIS*, OECD Publishing, http://dx.doi.org/10.1787/9789264123540-en.

Wahlstrom, K.L. and K.S. Louis (2008), "How teachers experience principal leadership: The roles of professional community, trust, efficacy, and shared responsibility", *Educational Administration Quarterly*, Vol. 44, pp. 458-495.

Wayne, A.J. et al. (2008), "Experimenting with teacher professional development: Motives and methods", *Educational Researcher*, Vol. 37/8, pp. 469-479.

Wininger, S.R. and P.M. Birkholz (2013), "Sources of instructional feedback, job satisfaction, and basic psychological needs", *Innovative Higher Education*, Vol. 38, pp. 159-170.

Chapter 4

INNOVATING TO CREATE 21ST-CENTURY LEARNING ENVIRONMENTS

Innovation in education is not just a matter of putting more technology into more classrooms; it is about changing approaches to teaching so that students acquire the skills they need to thrive in competitive global economies. Based on the OECD study, Innovative Learning Environments, this chapter describes how some schools are regrouping teachers, regrouping learners, rescheduling learning, and changing pedagogical approaches – and the mix of those approaches – to provide better teaching for better learning.

Chapter 4
Innovating to create 21st-century learning environments

Given the pace and scale of change in the 21st century, there is increasing pressure for individuals and societies to be adaptable and continually learning. Education systems must equip young people with the skills and competencies that allow them to engage with and participate in the rapidly-changing world of today and tomorrow. Are the environments in which students – of all ages – learn sufficiently innovative to keep up with this challenging agenda?

This chapter draws on the Innovative Learning Environments (ILE) study carried out by the OECD. It focuses on innovative ways of organising learning with the aim of positively influencing education reform. The study concludes that schools and education systems will be most powerful and effective when they:

- Make learning central, encourage engagement, and be where learners come to understand themselves as learners.
- Ensure that learning is social and often collaborative.
- Are highly attuned to learners' motivations and the importance of emotions.
- Are acutely sensitive to individual differences, including in prior knowledge.
- Are demanding of each learner, but do not overload students with work.
- Use assessments consistent with their aims, emphasising formative feedback.
- Promote horizontal connectedness across activities and subjects, in and outside of school.

The study also concludes that three additional features and cycles need to be developed in order to implement these principles: a strong focus on, and innovation within, the "pedagogical cores" of schools and other environments; leadership, at all levels, to promote 21st-century learning; and engagement with others, through networks and partnerships, to extend boundaries and build professional capacity.

Innovating using the "pedagogic core" at the heart of schools and learning environments means transforming organisational relationships and dynamics to make them relevant for the 21st century. In many cases, this means rethinking the kinds of organisational patterns that are the backbone of most schools today: the lone teacher; the classroom separated from other classrooms, each with its own teacher; the familiar class schedule and bureaucratic units; and the traditional approaches to teaching and classroom organisation. This is not to suggest that all schools across OECD countries strictly follow this pattern; many no longer fit this profile at all. The case studies described below have systematically rethought many of these practices and have created new learning environments by regrouping teachers, regrouping learners, rescheduling learning, and/or changing pedagogical approaches and the mix of those approaches.

REGROUPING EDUCATORS AND TEACHERS

The case studies highlight three main reasons for abandoning the conventional one-teacher-per-group-of-learners format. First, there are the benefits of collaborative planning, working together and shared professional development strategies (i.e. teamwork as an organisational norm). Second, team teaching allows for a wider variety of teaching options. Third, teamwork can benefit certain groups of learners who might otherwise not get the attention they need when only one teacher is in charge.

In some of the cases, collaboration might be described as part of the general culture of the learning organisation:

> Teaching teams are cross-curricular and complementary at *Lakes South Morang P-9 School (Victoria, Australia)*, with team members planning and teaching together, as well as coaching one another. To support this, a collaborative data-storage system is available for sharing documentation, assessments, etc. Experienced team teachers also engage in coaching other teachers on various teaching approaches that cater to different learning styles.
>
> *Lobdeburgschule, Jena (Thuringia, Germany)*: Twenty years ago, teachers introduced teamwork as a structural element. Organisational and pedagogical themes, as well as learning and working practices, are discussed in the teams. In the early 1990s, they established the "morning circle", when all students gather to discuss different aspects of school life.
>
> Teachers in the *Quality Learning Center and Enquiry Zone, Mordialloc College (Victoria, Australia)* used to "teach to the text", according to the assistant principal, within single, closed-door classrooms. This has changed. Now teachers open up their classrooms and work in teams to model and share good practice – not only with their colleagues, but also with students and the broader community.

> **Box 4.1. Desirable features of contemporary learning environments**
>
> Innovate using the elements and dynamics of the "pedagogical core" in line with design strategies and the "learning principles".
>
> Become a "formative organisation" through strong design strategies and corresponding leadership supported by learning information richness and effective feedback channels.
>
> Open up to partnerships to grow and sustain their social and professional capital.
>
> Promote 21st-century effectiveness through application of the ILE learning principles.
>
> Source: OECD (2013a), *Innovative Learning Environments*, http://dx.doi.org/10.1787/9789264203488-en.

Collaborative planning, orchestration and professional development

The collaborative process of team teaching encourages informal reflection and feedback. When teachers work together regularly, collaboration becomes a tool for recording, learning and sharing good practice. This is very much in line with the development of "professional learning communities" for teachers, which collaboratively analyse pedagogy and lesson content in order to continually refine practice.

> Professional learning is a priority in the *Community Learning Campus (CLC), Olds High School (Alberta, Canada)*. Much of the professional learning is embedded in daily activities, such as team teaching, curriculum building (multidisciplinary teams of teachers working collaboratively to design an integrated, multidisciplinary programme of study), collaborative lesson planning and team meetings. Teachers also attend professional learning days scheduled by the school or the district.
>
> An important aspect in *CEIP, Andalucía (Spain)* is the collaborative work of both teachers and students. Adults in the school (teachers, families and volunteers) are organised into working groups, commissions, meetings, the Teachers' Assembly, etc. This teamwork culture is also present inside the classroom, where several adults often work together in the same class.
>
> At *Jenaplan-Schule, Jena (Thuringia, Germany)*, teachers collaborate in regular meetings, such as team conferences with teachers from all classes/grades. In the weekly team meetings, teachers discuss important topics for the forthcoming week and develop the subject matter, materials and methods to be used.

> *With all my teachers, if they don't collaborate with each other, if they don't learn together, if they don't de-privatise their classrooms, then we won't be able to reach the level of deep learning and engagement that we are striving to achieve. It takes everyone working together all the time, learning together every day.*
>
> The Principal, Community Learning Campus (CLC), Olds High School (Alberta, Canada)

Regrouping teachers to introduce different mixes of learning and pedagogy

Several of the case studies refer to team teaching that allows for different approaches by two or more educators working together with a large group of learners. It is worth noting that, in education, small is not always preferable to large. Large groups of students may sometimes be taught together in lecture mode, then broken down into smaller groups for other styles of teaching.

> Instead of deploying one teacher in a 30-student classroom, in certain subjects the *Cramlington Learning Village (United Kingdom)* features two teachers for a 60-student class. This adds flexibility to the class schedule and allows teachers to split students into groups in any way that suits their needs, such as for parallel or differentiated instruction. It also allows them to run cross-disciplinary sessions, such as an enquiry facilitated by a science and media teacher. The result is that teachers across many disciplines can build flexibility at no extra cost. The process of team teaching can also help to model and release the creative energies of collaboration, resulting in new and novel ways of orchestrating learning that are engaging to learners.

> In *CEIP (Spain)*, the entire class of students is regularly divided into groups of four or five. The lesson comprises activities that each last 15 or 20 minutes, and are accompanied by a teacher or another adult. Once the time devoted to one activity has finished, the adults rotate to another group, so that they spend some time with all the groups at every lesson. Each group carries out a different activity, but the general subject matter of all activities is the same.
>
> Team teaching is used in almost all lessons at *Europäische Volksschule Dr. Leopold Zechner (Vienna, Austria)*. Many of these teachers speak the same language as the immigrant students in the classes.

Team teaching to target specific groups of learners

Specific groups of learners who might not get the attention they need in large-group classes often benefit from team teaching.

> Having two teachers in the classroom in *Europaschule (Linz, Austria)* allows for a more personal level of attention. For example, one teacher concentrates on the subject matter and explains tasks, while the special needs teacher primarily focuses on social issues, supports group-building processes and attends to those who need special attention.
>
> Similarly, in the *Hauptschule (St. Marein bei Graz, Austria)*, students are taught in mixed-age classes, including some students with special needs. Instead of streaming students into ability groups, teacher teams apply within-class differentiation, alternating between basic teaching for the whole class and add-on content for highly motivated students or extra support for less-motivated students.
>
> Three to five teachers work with *Dobbantó (Springboard)* students *(Hungary)* on an ongoing basis; two of them are present together in the classroom 40% of the time. Generally, there are three teachers working with the group in the humanities, natural sciences and a vocational field, respectively, with at least one of the three having experience in teaching students with special education needs.
>
> Instead of taking low-achieving students out of the classroom in *CEIP (Spain)*, another teacher joins the class during the two hours each day when flexible groups are organised. As a result, there is less misconduct in classes and low-achievers improve their academic performance.

Enhanced visibility

When teachers work together in teams, they all learn from each other's techniques and practices because they can finally see those practices (enhanced visibility); they are no longer hidden behind a closed classroom door. The visibility is enhanced even further when this becomes organisation-wide rather than just among individual collaborating colleagues (Hattie, 2009). While this practice might be unnerving to teachers at first, it is inherent in the nature of innovation to disrupt established habits before the innovation is integrated and becomes accepted in organisational practice.

> Teachers at the *John Monash Science School (Victoria, Australia)* identified the benefits of "knowing what others are doing", and therefore learning from one another, as well as "having a stronger sense of what the students are learning" and the ways in which richer connections could be made between different areas of learning. This was a new way of working for teachers, traditionally used to closed-off private areas and personal desks.
>
> The Distance Learning Classroom in *Lok Sin Tong Leung Wong Wai Fong Memorial School (Hong Kong-China)* gives students the opportunity to learn from their counterparts in different schools, and enables teachers to observe lessons and exchange information with their peers who are not physically "on site". The Smart Classroom is an advanced technological classroom that allows teachers to use a wide variety of media in their teaching. It also serves as a live link with other partner schools.

REGROUPING LEARNERS

One of the most common ways in which the innovative learning environments discussed here regroup learners is by mixing older and younger learners together. When a school is very small, such mixing is inevitable.

Grouping together learners of different ages

There is a variety of reasons offered by the case-study schools for grouping together learners of different ages: as a stimulus to learning; as a way of encouraging diversity and contacts that would otherwise be unlikely to develop; to enable peer teaching; and as a way of reducing bullying and fostering good social relations.

Innovating to create 21st-century learning environments

In the Danish *Lisbjerg School,* there are two large groups composed of students whose ages span three years (6 to 9 years and 10 to 13 years). The students are also organised into smaller groups of 12, which are also mixed in terms of age. Teaching is differentiated and alternates between working within the bigger and the smaller groups. Every student follows an individualised learning path (called "the child's storyline"), and documents work in different portfolios.

In the *Community of Learners Network (British Columbia, Canada),* teachers work within and between the walls of the traditional school structures to create innovative approaches to teaching and learning. For example, in elementary (K-7) classrooms, where students are placed in cohorts based on age, teachers collaborate across grades. They have shifted the physical structures and the learning structures to enhance collaboration among students of different ages, and they have shifted the power structures to include students as key resources in the education of their peers – and their teachers.

In the *Presteheia (Kristianssand, Norway),* learner groups vary in age and size but tend to be between 33 and 54 students. Time in the large mixed groups is used to build relations among children who would otherwise not socialise. This reduces the incidence of bullying at school and increases feelings of security and confidence. It also makes it easier for students to find someone with whom they can have a trusting relation because they can choose among more students. Teachers and other staff are deployed flexibly.

> *For me the most important aspect of student learning in mixed-age groups is that this kind of learning gives the student a learning "push". It always leads to success. The children gain a lot of strength from this success, and it is also true for those learning areas where they are not as capable. These learning boosts, kindled by these successes, are irreplaceable.*
>
> Teacher, Jenaplan-Schule, Jena (Thuringia, Germany)

Some of the case studies are very small schools with mixed-grade classes. They intentionally use the heterogeneity of their students as the basis for an individualised education, to encourage integration and autonomous learning.

Gesamtschule Schupberg (Boll, Switzerland) is a small school with a multigrade classroom composed of students of varying cognitive and physical abilities. The school emphasises the heterogeneity of the student group, and regards the heterogeneous student body as a stimulating and motivating influence on the children's social and cognitive development.

All 20 students, from grade 1 to 9, in the *One-room School, Gesamtschule Lindental (Boll, Switzerland)* are placed in one mixed-age class. Although students are assigned to a certain grade, learning activities are adapted to their current level of development, allowing for gifted students to be challenged and for weaker students to develop greater self-confidence as learners.

Smaller groups within the larger groups

Several of the innovation sites operate with a "house" system that offers a more manageable organisational unit and stimulates more "family-oriented" engagement among students.

Subscribing to the principle that learning is a social endeavour, the *Community Learning Campus (CLC), Olds High School (Alberta, Canada)* is both physically and programmatically organised into four learning communities, called "quads". The quads provide a range of learning settings for a wide variety of groupings and configurations of students. The quads are each named according to a colour: Red, Green, Blue and Gold. The Red Quad is composed of grade-9 students. It is the only quad that contains a single grade. The other three quads include a mix of grade-10, -11 and -12 students. Students remain in the same quad, with the same group of teachers, throughout their three years in high school.

A key part of the collaborative environment in the *Australian Science and Mathematics School (South Australia, Australia)* is the Tutor Group Programme. Each student is a member of the same multiyear group for the duration of his or her time at the school. The Tutor Group meets daily for 40 minutes. A key role of the Tutor Group is to "ensure that students feel a sense of belonging within the school" and to "provide care and guidance through strong student-teacher relationships".

> At *Colegio Karol Cardenal de Cracovia (Santiago, Chile)*, the unit is not the "house" or "family" or "quad", but the "ministry", as in a national or regional government. In each ministry there is a student minister, counsellor teacher, parent minister, chiefs of communal departments, mayor of the class and deputy secretary.
>
> The "president" is elected during political campaigns that involve voting boxes and election monitors. The student who wins the largest share of votes becomes president of the school government, and the student who wins the next highest number votes becomes the secretary-general to the president.

Co-operative learning is a prominent feature in many of the innovative sites. In some cases, it is more formalised through the establishment of learner groups that are considerably smaller than the houses or tutor groups described above. In the case of the Hong Kong-China school, there is a deliberate strategy of mixing abilities in small working groups.

> *Lok Sin Tong Leung Wong Wai Fong Memorial School (Hong Kong-China)* has restructured all classes in primary grades 1-6, dividing students into small groups, normally of around 3 or 4 pupils. These heterogeneous groups are formed according to students' academic performance. Each group is made up of both more able and less able students. The heterogeneity of the groups enhances co-operative learning in which students work together to maximise their own and each other's learning.
>
> *Mevo'ot HaNegev Kibbutz Shoval (Israel)* operates with a projects-based pedagogy, with projects taking place around a specific problem or question that can be theoretical, practical or both. The learners divide into workgroups of 3-4 students each, and then examine a topic or a sub-topic from the wider subject.

RESCHEDULING LEARNING: INNOVATING WITH HOW TIME IS USED

Schedules structure the school day, week or cycle; the school "timetable" provides a central organising tool in schools the world over. Many educators still see time primarily in quantitative terms, i.e. as something one has more or less of, with the effectiveness of teaching directly related to it. But with innovative ways of using time, time is regarded in more qualitative terms.

Timetables, flexibility and time use

The distribution and planning of activities over time is a familiar part of school life. A number of the innovative learning environments described here have moved in the direction of organising learning into fewer, longer periods, partly for greater flexibility, but particularly in order to enhance the opportunities for deeper learning.

> *Mevo'ot HaNegev Kibbutz Shoval (Israel)* has a shorter school week (5 days) and longer lessons (60 minutes) than is customary in Israel, to allow students to engage more deeply in their lessons. The number of subjects covered per week was reduced from 8 to 4 or 5; the relationship between teachers and learners has become more personal; learning has been oriented towards understanding; studying has become more individual and autonomous; and teachers mentor and support the learners.
>
> Every day except Wednesday at *John Monash Science School (Victoria, Australia)* begins with a 15-minute tutorial group meeting. The timetable of the school operates on a four-period day, and a ten-day cycle. Each period is 75 minutes long so as to provide, as described by the principal, "opportunities for deep learning".
>
> The timetable at the *Community Learning Campus (CLC), Olds High School (Alberta, Canada)* consists of five 70-minute blocks with 10 minutes between classes. One of five blocks of time is known as Flex Period (flexible period). Students explained that they have time to eat and also enough time to work on homework or anything else they might wish to work on. They also have access to a teacher during this time.

As some of the schools in the case studies move away from the standard subject-based curriculum, it is not surprising to find that this is reflected in their timetables.

> In Spanish schools, time is organised according to subjects; but in the *Instituto Escuela Jacint Verdaguer* the timetable is based on methodology instead. The three areas into which the curriculum is organised are reflected in students' timetables and the "learning pyramid": 25% of the time is devoted to instrumental areas, 25% to personal work and autonomy, 40% to co-operative work, and the remaining 10% to intrapersonal work.

Innovating to create 21st-century learning environments

> The academic year lasts 36 weeks in *Dobbantó (Springboard) (Hungary)*, as in any other Hungarian vocational school, but the daily and weekly schedules are quite different. Approximately 60% of study time is devoted to general education and 40% is devoted to developing work-related competencies.

Many of the cases that were studied use time more flexibly than do traditional schools. Flexibility goes hand-in-hand with individualised learning plans and with education philosophies that aim to make schooling less bureaucratic.

> The *Europaschule (Austria)* has no school bell, since many believe the sound interrupts learning. Teachers start and end their lessons or break a double period when they consider it appropriate.
>
> Instead of the 45-minute rhythm and subject-oriented instruction normally found in the German school system, an open, adaptive form of instruction is applied in the *Jenaplan-Schule, Jena (Thuringia, Germany)*. Individual students have enough flexibility in their schedules and free time to work and learn at their own pace during the day, and to pursue their other interests, apply their creativity and develop their social skills. The goal is to have students understand themselves as active and independent learners who can enjoy the fruits of their efforts.

> *In Makor Chaim they do not believe in the rigid 45-minute lesson structure. (…) It is not a matter of how many words the teacher said or the students said, but whether learning took place. To make that happen one must induce processes similar to those that exist in the real world, where in addition to situations where grown-ups teach the young ones, there are also situations where people investigate, test and study in collaboration with colleagues.*
>
> Researcher, *Makor Chaim (Life source) – Yeshiva High School (Israel)*

Some of the innovative learning environments studied provide their students with the opportunity to "accelerate" their learning. There is international evidence that this leads to improved results (Hattie, 2009).

> At the *Australian Science and Mathematics School (South Australia, Australia)*, year-10 students may study subjects at year-11 or year-12 level, while year-12 students have the opportunity to take first-year courses at Flinders University as part of their year-12 studies. The school responds to the learning needs of its most motivated and gifted students by allowing them to self-pace their learning and do away with the confines of the traditional school year cycle.

Rituals can help to structure the school day and make it meaningful; they create routines of reflection or planning. Several of the innovation sites studied begin and conclude the school day or week with such a special moment. For example:

> In the *Projektschule Impuls, Rorschach (Bern, Switzerland)* the day begins with a "morning circle" when a "speaker-stone" is passed around and the children can talk about their feelings or thoughts. There is a regular structure to the day. Classes start with a foreign-language session, followed by group work based on learning plans. Afterwards there is a period of absolute quietness, timed by a sandglass that runs for 25 minutes while the students remain at their place and do not speak or walk around.
>
> The Multimedia Programme, including "The Morning Show", the CGPS Radio Show and Film-Making project, has become central to the *Courtenay Gardens Primary School (Victoria, Australia)*. The show is run each morning by a group of senior school learners who apply to do so and undertake appropriate training. It provides the school community with information about their day ahead, transmitted throughout the school at 9.00 a.m. on the television in each classroom, in the staffroom and at the entrance to the school, from a dedicated multimedia classroom. The show follows a structured storyboard that includes an overview of news around the school, including student and staff birthdays, teachers on yard duty, weather, a "maths minute", phone-ins from classrooms, and a film made by students.

Organised learning outside regular school hours

A number of the case-study learning environments systematically structure learning and support for their learners outside regular school hours. There are many more examples than those cited below, as all of those sites using virtual e-classrooms, for instance, have removed the close connection between face-to-face contact and organised learning.

> The Entre Amigos association in the *Polígono Sur* is responsible for organising extracurricular activities through an official tender process of the City Council of Seville. From 8 a.m., the selected organisations are in charge of the "Morning Classroom", developed to assist those whose parents go to work early in the morning, most of them at street markets. Evening extracurricular activities start at 3 p.m. and finish at 5 p.m., although *CEIP (Spain)* is normally open later.
>
> The *Lok Sin Tong Leung Wong Wai Fong Memorial School (Hong Kong-China)* has launched a number of activities for students before, during and after school. Those who need to be at school early can join the "Reading is Fun" programme, from 7:15 a.m. through most of the following hour. Students can choose different kinds of books to read and share afterwards. In addition to lunchtime activities, students can join the Student Gardener Team to look after the plants in the school garden and in the community garden during recess. Every afternoon, students have 40 minutes of self-study to work on their homework. There is also a two-hour period at the end of the school day for tutorial classes on academic and creative subjects.
>
> The *Enrichment Programmes, Rodica Primary School (Slovenia)* offers an array of artistic, research, international, linguistic and social activities that encourage creative thinking, constructivist education and diverse paths to knowledge. These complement the regular programme and are offered mostly outside of regular lesson time, in the afternoon or on Saturdays.

WIDENING PEDAGOGICAL REPERTOIRES

Innovative learning environments also work with different pedagogical approaches to expand teaching and learning. Many focus on inquiry approaches and collaborative work, both of which are critical for preparing students for future learning and for equipping students with 21st-century skills. These sites also take full advantage of the possibilities afforded by communication technologies. What is important are the *mixes* of pedagogical approaches. Innovation is not about using a single new teaching method or one kind of technology; it is about employing a combination of approaches, including direct teaching, and tools.

Inquiry learning

> *Inquiry and design-based approaches are an important way to nurture communication, collaboration, creativity, and deep thinking [but] Inquiry approaches to learning are challenging to implement. They are highly dependent on the knowledge and skills of the teachers engaged in trying to implement them... Teachers need time and a community to support their capacity to organise sustained project work. It takes significant pedagogical sophistication to manage extended projects in classrooms so as to maintain a focus on "doing with understanding" rather than "doing for the sake of doing".*
>
> Brigid Barron and Linda Darling-Hammond, in their contribution to the OECD review, *The Nature of Learning: Using Research to Inspire Practice* (2010: 215)

In many of the innovative cases studied, students engage in project-based learning. They are encouraged to acquire knowledge while practising skills, like hypothesis generation, scientific inquiry, self-monitoring and (sometimes online) literary analysis. Some sites have shifted from subject-specific teaching towards more interdisciplinary learning that links knowledge and skills from several subject areas.

> The *Jenaplan-Schule, Jena (Thuringia, Germany)* distinguishes among learner group instruction (music, arts, sports, handicrafts/woodworking, etc., and social studies), learner group work, and learner group projects in nature, geography/history, German and ethics/religion. In all learner groups, the project work, scheduled for 100 minutes three times a week, is the central working form.
>
> "Problem-Based Learning" is an important part of students' work in natural sciences, social sciences and technology at *Instituto Escuela Jacint Verdaguer (Spain)*. All such work is planned as a team and carried out either co-operatively or individually. Understanding a problem is considered to be the first step on the path to finding a solution to the problem. The organisation of learning spaces, the timetable, activities, trips and workshops are based on this methodology.
>
> At *Matthew Moss High School, Innovation Unit (England, United Kingdom)*, student teams work one day per week on a research project. The teachers first introduce a challenge, which can vary from launching an egg as high as possible and returning it to earth without breaking or responding to a natural disaster, to investigating family histories of migration. The students then gather information about the topic, write a research proposal, and, after the proposal is approved by the teacher, conduct the research throughout the school year. In the process, they are free to organise their own research, while the teachers act as facilitators who present in-time lessons or suggest additional sources of knowledge.

The inquiry cycle method used in the British Columbian example below formalises the stages of inquiry into the cycle as shown in the figure.

> In the *Community of Learners Network (British Columbia, Canada)*, educators design broad inquiry questions that encompass a range of learning intentions. Background knowledge is developed through direct instruction and a series of information-gathering collaborative processes, such as research, "jigsaw", literature circles, information circles, field experiences and guest presentations. A prominent feature of this phase is a series of "circle meetings" where students' learning is co-constructed and facilitated in small groups. Reflective writing and representations of evolving understanding, using mind maps, follow the small group meetings.
>
> **Figure 4.1**
> **The Community of Learners Network classroom inquiry cycle**
>
> - Engage students in broad inquiry question
> - Develop background knowledge
> - Coach to personal inquiry question and action plan
> - Support through peer coaching and ongoing check-ins
> - Reflect on learning
> - Showcase to Community
> - Develop Community of Learners culture
>
> Source: OECD (2012), Inventory Case Study "Community of Learners Network", www.oecd.org/edu/ceri/50301622.pdf.
>
> After this phase, the students are coached to articulate their own inquiry questions that fit within the larger inquiry question. As they pursue their individual inquiries, they often facilitate learning experiences for their classmates. Ongoing progress is supported through multilevel feedback circles that rely on self, peer and teacher support. The inquiry process is followed by a celebration of learning, called a Learning Showcase, where families, fellow students and community members are invited to share in the learning experience. Once the inquiry circle is completed a new one begins, following the same sequencing of activities. This allows the students to become more autonomous in their learning and gradually take on more challenging inquiry projects as they progress.

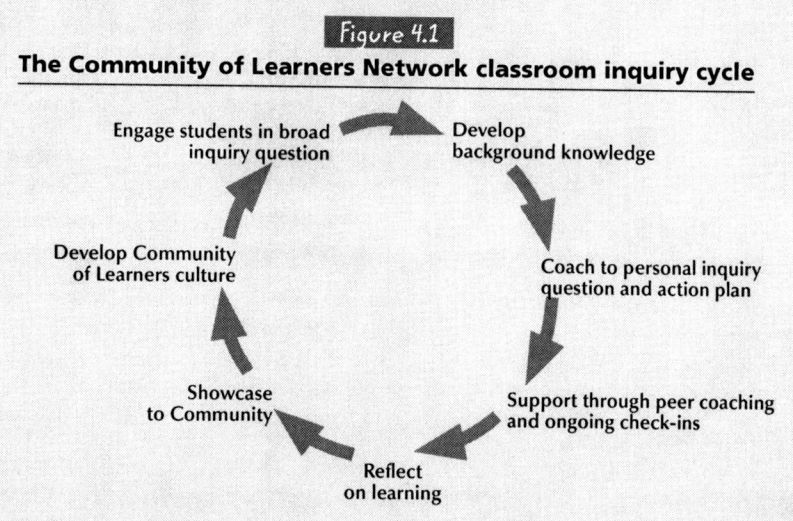

Authentic learning

It is a common feature of many innovative learning environments to make the learning experience authentic and meaningful by engaging students with real-life problems, offering hands-on experiences, and incorporating the students' historical, natural and cultural environment into learning activities. Central to authentic teaching are "real-life" problems, which are interesting to students because they are more relevant, complex and challenging than simplified problems designed by educators, and because they are more closely linked to the development of 21st-century skills.

> In the *Centre for Studies on Design at Monterrey (CEDIM), The Atelier of Ideas, Monterrey (Nuevo León, Mexico)*, the college co-operates with enterprises and institutions that submit "real-world" projects that student teams complete – from brainstorming to final evaluation, with instructors acting as counsellors in this process. There are three major steps: project design – coming up with a plan to bring the project to fruition; collaborative work – working together to optimise the process and the outcomes; and evaluation – by the teacher, peers, the individual student and the external agency that came up with the project proposal.
>
> The three-year practical building and living project at *Breidablikk Lower Secondary School (Norway)* involves students building houses on a 1:20 scale. Students get to play the role of builder, gardener, electrician, bank employee, real estate agent and others. To this end, the school co-operates with representatives of different businesses. Students use the same digital tools that architects use, and houses are furnished with electricity and handmade furniture. All designs must be environmentally sustainable.

Work on real-life problems often goes together with hands-on experience. At a few sites, hands-on learning involves inviting native speakers of the languages students are learning into the classroom – or through videoconferencing – for face-to-face conversations, or letting students participate in international events where they can hear and speak the languages they are studying.

Hands-on experience may also entail running a small business, such as producing and selling homemade products or working on problems posed by external customers. The students naturally gain experience in such activities as marketing, accounting and customer service, but also in organisation, co-ordination and team work.

> The *Mypolonga Primary School (South Australia, Australia)* has a student-organised shop in which the students sell homemade products, and products commissioned from the local community, to visitors and tourists. All classes are involved in business, craft and tourism, and senior students along with a junior trainee operate the shop one day per week. Students rotate through a series of tasks in the shop, acquiring language, mathematics, art, craft and hospitality skills along the way.

Authentic learning activities often involve aspects of the students' immediate environment. These allow students to explore the world around them and learn about the cultural and historical heritage of the place where they live.

> *Liikkeelle! (On the Move!), Heureka, Finnish Science Centre (Finland)* encourages students to examine everyday settings from the perspective of natural sciences. Activities include investigating air quality and noise levels with the guidance of the relevant experts and authorities. Students place a measuring device near their school, work with a centre for natural-science teaching for analysis, process the data and publish results in an interactive map on an online learning platform. They then discuss the results with students from other schools and with a wide network of experts.

Authentic learning often involves several rounds of review and revision toward a polished result, which may be an exhibition, a stage performance or a portfolio. When students can present their work to a real audience, it becomes a source of public learning and celebration (Barron and Darling-Hammond, 2010). Working towards a final performance also motivates students to achieve genuine mastery because real audiences demand coherent presentations and a high level of understanding. Presentations are also learning events in themselves: setting them up involves skills like organising group efforts and communicating effectively with an audience. Once again, the relationship with 21st-century competencies is clear.

> In the *CEDIM, The Atelier of Ideas, Monterrey (Nuevo León, Mexico)*, students present the projects they have been working on – all of which respond to real enterprise and community demands – in front of local enterprises and public and/or private institutions. By doing so, the assessment of their work becomes much more authentic and meaningful to students.
>
> The Showcase is a celebration that completes each inquiry cycle, and has come to be seen as an essential element of the learning process (*Community of Learners Network, British Columbia, Canada*). Classmates, school administrators, families and community members are all invited to view the products that the students have created, and to discuss their learning experiences with them.
>
> *Europäische Volksschule Dr. Leopold Zechner (Austria)* practices a special performance assessment called "commented performance portfolio" up to the third grade. Twice a year students present their achievements to parents and teachers in a detailed conversation that lasts around 30 minutes. Students present work they have done and answer teachers' questions or demonstrate learning by solving problems they feel confident they can tackle in front of their parents.

The pedagogical possibilities in "technology-rich" environments

While technology is certainly not a prerequisite for project-based work, it can be highly facilitating (OECD, 2010). Technology can provide the tools necessary to complete an investigation. Digital cameras and video recorders can collect real-time data, while laptops can offer easy access to online searches and mobile computing. Technology can offer a platform for inquiry-based learning, providing a collaborative working space for individual learners, groups of learners, and classes or networks of learners. Technology can be the mechanism upon which inquiry-based learning is built, such as through game-based learning or online simulations, structuring inquiry-based learning in an engaging and relevant way (Groff, 2012).

Engagement and motivation, student-driven learning and inquiry, interactivity and collaboration, personalisation and flexibility, may all be enhanced with technology – but all are possible without it. Still, some forms of learning rely heavily on technology.

Box 4.2. Technology-dependent approaches to teaching and learning

Specific complex learning experiences: For example, with new advances in simulation technology, every student can have the chance to dissect a pig's heart – something that would be very difficult in reality.

Distant communication and collaboration: Now, learners and schools can easily connect to share information and collaborate via free tools, like Skype, or a group of students interested in studying the migration patterns of a certain bird can join an online affinity group and be mentored by a leading expert.

Mobility and access to extensive materials: Technology now brings access to educational materials and experiences of a richness and kind that previously would not have been possible or accessible only in discrete locations such as a university library.

Source: Groff, J. (2012), *Technology-Rich Innovative Learning Environments*, www.oecd.org/edu/ceri/Technology-Rich%20Innovative%20Learning%20Environments%20by%20Jennifer%20Groff.pdf.

A specific learning practice that recurs in many of the cases studied is film production – which cannot be done without technology. Students go through the complete process of filmmaking, from idea generation, to planning, storyboarding and scripting, to production and final presentation.

At *Miwon Elementary School (Gyeonggi-do, Korea)*, volunteer fifth- and sixth-grade students choose topics of interest to them and their parents and produce a film. One of the films produced portrayed problems arising in a multicultural society and possible solutions. The project was supported by "Changshi", a Korean creative filmmaking association. Since 2006, these student films have won a number of awards, including the Youth Film Festival Award and the 7th Korea Video Award. Participating students have been invited to a multicultural education seminar and to the 7th Korea Youth Film Festival.

In the *Community/School Film Festival at the Manchester Primary School (Victoria, Australia)*, the objective is to engage primary school students with the curriculum by encouraging them to make short films. Filming is used as a cross-curricular activity involving flexible movement around the school and group negotiation, and is regarded as a tool through which students can demonstrate their understanding. Teachers and film technicians support the students, and the project culminates in an authentic film festival, fostering an exchange of resources and expertise.

> We also do a weekly programme with the students of the 6th year, which is called 'OndAventura' (WaveAdventure). The idea of the radio programme is to have a participative space where students can develop the linguistic skill: they express themselves, they have to prepare it, write the script ... and it is supervised by a teacher. The radio workshop takes place in a radio station located in the school, which, like all the school premises, is available to the neighbourhood.
>
> Head of Studies, *CEIP* (Spain)

Mixes of pedagogies

> In a well-designed environment, there may well be plenty of occasion for direct instruction as one of a range of methods for introducing and pacing content, to be used in combination with other, less directed approaches (....) The focus on learning environments as patterned mixes of different learning activities that take place in context over time facilitates the insight that the learners need to experience a range, not a single method or pedagogy.
>
> Istance and Dumont (2010: 328)

The orchestration of learning within the environment is complex, involving many decisions, often taken by teachers working collaboratively or with others in the learning leadership, about when and where and with whom particular pedagogies are appropriate, and how these should be modulated over time. In all of the examples below, part of the day involves whole-group, teacher-led activities, mixed in with other types of teaching and learning.

> In the *Lobdeburgschule (Thuringia, Germany)*, a typical week for a grade-1 student starts with the Monday "morning circle" where various topics are discussed. Then, learners work on their individual plans with partners, sometimes with the help of the teacher and using a range of different worksheets and prepared materials for support ("free work"). Then, it is the "epochal projects" session, which is project-based. Students work for about a week on a single theme that includes different subjects and topics of the Thuringian curriculum. At the beginning of the project, the teacher provides core information; questions about the theme are developed, and sometimes small working groups are formed. The results are presented at the end of the week. Subject-oriented lessons follow, but students are more free to direct their learning in these lessons. The school week ends with the group "final circle" on Friday afternoon.
>
> At the *Mordialloc College (Victoria, Australia)*, the daily expedition time (11.00 a.m.-1.00 p.m.) provides opportunities for workshops and student conferences related to the substantive curriculum content, as well as embedded aspects of literacy and numeracy. Guides also hold workshops on areas that address the specific needs of students. These are the key points of direct instruction for students and are generally held for groups of 15 or more students.
>
> Coursework at *Jenaplan-Schule, Jena (Thuringia, Germany)* includes mandatory subjects, but it also demands a high degree of development and discovery by individual students.
>
> In the *Instituto Escuela Jacint Verdaguer (Spain)*, teachers are still regarded as the best source of information on reading, writing and arithmetic, and they perform that knowledge-transmission function for learners who would not be able to discover core concepts by themselves or in a short time.
>
> Traditional methods of teaching can be complemented by e-classrooms for acquiring and strengthening knowledge, as well as for assessment *(Internet Classroom, Kkofja Loka Primary School, Slovenia)*. Teachers' learning materials, prepared in advance, are collected in one place within the e-classroom where they may be used directly without downloading. Instruction via e-classroom takes place through an interactive whiteboard and portable tablets. E-classrooms allow for individual feedback after completed work or activity, with messages or a grade or a knowledge test given before progression to the next level.

Even in learning environments that have deliberately sought to move away from conventional forms of teaching and organisation, there are particular subjects for which those more conventional approaches are judged to be the most suitable even if, in these cases, teachers are always looking to encourage more active engagement among their students. The mix of pedagogies may be realised through the different media and settings used, as when e-classroom work is integrated into the larger menu of teaching and learning options. It may also stem from teachers' preferences and choices as part of the wider orchestration of learning. Again, these innovative learning environments have not simply replaced one approach or methodology with another, but rather use a wide array of approaches, all of which are aligned with the broader learning strategy.

POLICY IMPLICATIONS

The pedagogical changes outlined in this chapter imply that:

- all the participants develop the expertise, attitudes and skills to engage in these forms of advanced teaching and learning;
- the organisational and systemic structures and infrastructure, including technological infrastructure, permit innovative teaching and learning environments to flourish;
- new competencies and expert knowledge are acquired and shared collaboratively, horizontally as well as vertically, within formal systems;
- learning that takes place outside formal schooling is recognised, and new partnerships and hybrids are created to allow this to happen;
- students, themselves, are active partners in learning; and
- the broader climate and culture support innovation.

The policy implications of the innovative learning environments described in this chapter may be summed up around a series of Cs: creating communities and building capacities; collaboration and communication; conducive conditions and climates; and coherence.

Create communities and build capacities

Micro-level organisational routines that ensure that learning remains the core of all school activity are promising ways forward. They set out to erode the "grammars", or organisational cultures, in which teachers work largely in isolation from one another and are focused more on maintaining the institutional status quo and less on optimising student learning (Tyack and Cuban, 1995). Such routines aim to disrupt these "grammars" through collaborative activity, observation and change. Each teacher in the team becomes used to systematic observation from their colleagues, and all engage in a collective discussion of how to improve teaching and learning. Examples include Lesson Study and Learning Study, associated particularly with Japan and Hong Kong-China and as summarised in Cheng and Mo (2013). They also include the "kernel routines" proposed by Lauren Resnick and her colleagues in *The Nature of Learning: Using Research to Inspire Practice*, which gives examples of collective "learning walks" (Resnick et al, 2010). There is a clear policy role in fostering the knowledge, behaviours and support that enable such routines to flourish: by making information about exemplars widely available, encouraging appropriate professional learning and networking around such routines, and developing the related skills among teachers and school leaders.

> *When chosen purposefully and implemented well, new organisational routines can function as powerful instruments for transforming school practice. Resnick and Spillane (2006) used the term "kernel routine" to denote an organisational routine that has the potential for transforming school practice by "seeding" and "propagating" new forms of practice in schools(...) Kernel routines work by connecting and weaving together other organisational routines in the organisation. Rather than attempting to drive out current practices, the kernel routine recruits and "re-purposes" the familiar ways of doing things... [with] clear articulation of the steps in the routine, the rationale for these steps, and the requirements of each one. This calls for training procedures and a set of tools and artefacts for performing the routine.*
>
> Resnick et al. (2010: 293)

Collaborate and communicate

Technology contributes to all the different components, relationships, partnerships and principles that are integral to learning environments (Istance and Kools, 2013). The role of technology in organising learning data and feedback is central if schools are to become formative organisations. Distributed leadership may very well depend on technology for communication and collaboration, as might teacher learning using online materials, collaborative platforms or social media. Technology is often integral to building partnerships and sharing experiences and knowledge. This is particularly obvious and significant in networking with other learning environments.

Policies to foster innovation in how technology can be used in education require sophisticated approaches to digital materials and technological infrastructure. At the same time, the mere presence of technology in the classroom, in the form of computers or tablets in a school or in mobile phones in the pockets of learners, is not, by itself, sufficient. Education still must be "learning-centred", not "technology-driven" (Mayer, 2010).

Ideally, all primary stakeholders should join together so that the drive to innovate in education is felt throughout the education system, not only in isolated areas. Teachers can play a crucial role as catalysts for change, and other partners can be included as well. Michael Fullan (2011) describes many of the traditional reform instruments as the "wrong drivers" – accountability pressures, individual teacher- and leadership-quality approaches, technology, and fragmented strategies. According to Fullan, these do not lead to culture change and re-professionalisation; often they have a demotivating effect on teachers and school leaders. Instead, the "right" drivers include focusing on the learning-teaching-assessment nexus, social capital to build the profession, and matching pedagogy to technology.

Twenty-first-century learning environments should constantly try to create wider partnerships and connections. Partners bolster the education workforce, resources and sites for learning as a kind of "capital investment" – the social, intellectual and professional capital on which a thriving learning organisation depends (Hargreaves and Fullan, 2012). This is even more critical when resources are scarce, when more is expected to be done with less.

Create conditions conducive to innovation

Strong leadership is essential for supporting 21st-century learning (OECD, 2013b). Such leadership should be exercised at the micro level, in schools, then extend beyond the school through a web of networks and partnerships, and out to the wider education system itself. Change should be informed by evidence. Just as formative feedback should be integral to individual classes, so should it permeate the education system as a whole. Information about the learning taking place should be fed back to the different stakeholders, and incorporated into revised strategies for learning and further innovation. This means that processes for self-evaluation should be in place and knowledge should be shared. It also means that the knowledge base should be continually developed through meaningful research that engages the worlds of policy and practice. However, "information richness" about learning strategies, students and learning outcomes will quickly become information overload unless that information is converted into meaningful and actionable knowledge.

Developing the "meso" level through diverse networking and partnership arrangements is critical for developing more innovative learning environments. While this depends on local action, it has implications for policy through the creation of knowledge and information, incentives, capacity building, and appropriate governance arrangements so these networks can be developed. To create an environment conducive to innovation in education at the system level, the networks, strategies and connections at the "meso" level must thrive.

Ensure coherence

The complexity of contemporary learning systems, and the need to engage those most involved in teaching and learning on the ground, mean that top-down governance is often inappropriate. Thus, policy should help to create the conditions and climates that foster collaboration and build capacity. Learning-focused networks and communities of practice should be supported, and coherence with overarching education strategies should be ensured so that accountability demands do not work against the kind of innovative improvements described above.

But there is also a clear policy leadership role to be played as well. Many effective strategies depend on government design and leadership. Ministries and education agencies provide the legitimacy and the system-wide perspective to push innovation. Ideally, leadership from the local level, from networks and partnerships, and from education authorities at central and local levels should all be working together to create responsive 21st-century learning systems.

> **Note regarding Israel**
> The statistical data for Israel are supplied by and under the responsibility of the relevant Israeli authorities. The use of such data by the OECD is without prejudice to the status of the Golan Heights, East Jerusalem and Israeli settlements in the West Bank under the terms of international law.

References

Barron, B. and L. Darling-Hammond (2010), "Prospects and challenges for inquiry-based approaches to learning", in H. Dumont, D. Istance and F. Benavides (eds.), *The Nature of Learning: Using Research to Inspire Practice*, Educational Research and Innovation, OECD Publishing, Paris, http://dx.doi.org/10.1787/9789264086487-en.

Cheng, E.C. and M.L. Lo (2013). "Learning Study: its origins, operationalisation, and implications", *OECD Education Working Papers*, No. 94, OECD Publishing, Paris, http://dx.doi.org/10.1787/5k3wjp0s959p-en.

Dumont, H., D. Istance and F. Benavides (eds.) (2010), *The Nature of Learning: Using Research to Inspire Practice*, Educational Research and Innovation, OECD Publishing, Paris, http://dx.doi.org/10.1787/9789264086487-en.

Fullan, M. (2011), "Choosing the wrong drivers for whole system reform", *Seminar Series Paper* 204, Centre for Strategic Education, Melbourne.

Groff, J. (2012), *Technology-Rich Innovative Learning Environments*, OECD, Paris, www.oecd.org/edu/ceri/Technology-Rich%20Innovative%20Learning%20Environments%20by%20Jennifer%20Groff.pdf.

Hattie, J. (2009), *Visible Learning: A Synthesis of over 800 Meta-Analyses Related to Student Achievement*, Routledge, London.

Hargreaves, A. and M. Fullan (2012), *Professional Capital: Transforming Teaching in Every School*, Teachers College Press, London and New York, NY.

Istance, D. and M. Kools (2013), "Innovative learning environments as an integrating framework for technology in education", *European Journal of Education*, Vol. X, No. 1, pp 43-57.

Istance, D and H. Dumont (2010), "Future Directions for Learning Environments in the 21st Century", in H. Dumont, D. Istance and F. Benavides (eds.), *The Nature of Learning: Using Research to Inspire Practice*, Educational Research and Innovation, OECD Publishing, Paris, http://dx.doi.org/10.1787/9789264086487-en.

OECD (2013a), *Innovative Learning Environments*, Educational Research and Innovation, OECD Publishing, Paris, http://dx.doi.org/10.1787/9789264203488-en.

OECD (2013b), *Leadership for 21st Century Learning*, Educational Research and Innovation, OECD Publishing, Paris, http://dx.doi.org/10.1787/9789264205406-en.

OECD (2010), *Inspired by Technology, Driven by Pedagogy: A Systemic Approach to Technology-based School Innovations*, Educational Research and Innovation, OECD Publishing, Paris, http://dx.doi.org/10.1787/9789264094437-en.

Mayer, R.E. (2010), "Learning with Technology", in H. Dumont, D. Istance and F. Benavides (eds.), *The Nature of Learning: Using Research to Inspire Practice*, Educational Research and Innovation, OECD Publishing, Paris, http://dx.doi.org/10.1787/9789264086487-en.

Resnick, L.B., et al. (2010), "Implementing Innovation: from visionary models to everyday practice", in H. Dumont, D. Istance and F. Benavides (eds.), *The Nature of Learning: Using Research to Inspire Practice*, Educational Research and Innovation, OECD Publishing, Paris, http://dx.doi.org/10.1787/9789264086487-en.

Tyack, D. and L. Cuban (1995), *Tinkering Toward Utopia: A Century of Public School Reform*, Harvard University Press, Cambridge, MA.

ORGANISATION FOR ECONOMIC CO-OPERATION AND DEVELOPMENT

The OECD is a unique forum where governments work together to address the economic, social and environmental challenges of globalisation. The OECD is also at the forefront of efforts to understand and to help governments respond to new developments and concerns, such as corporate governance, the information economy and the challenges of an ageing population. The Organisation provides a setting where governments can compare policy experiences, seek answers to common problems, identify good practice and work to co-ordinate domestic and international policies.

The OECD member countries are: Australia, Austria, Belgium, Canada, Chile, the Czech Republic, Denmark, Estonia, Finland, France, Germany, Greece, Hungary, Iceland, Ireland, Israel, Italy, Japan, Korea, Luxembourg, Mexico, the Netherlands, New Zealand, Norway, Poland, Portugal, the Slovak Republic, Slovenia, Spain, Sweden, Switzerland, Turkey, the United Kingdom and the United States. The European Commission takes part in the work of the OECD.

OECD Publishing disseminates widely the results of the Organisation's statistics gathering and research on economic, social and environmental issues, as well as the conventions, guidelines and standards agreed by its members.

OECD PUBLISHING, 2, rue André-Pascal, 75775 PARIS CEDEX 16
(91 2015 02 1P) ISBN 978-92-64-23118-4 – 2015

CPSIA information can be obtained at www.ICGtesting.com
Printed in the USA
BVOW04s0626160116

433120BV00002B/14/P

9 789264 231184